Create Your
Life By Force

Create Your Life By Force

Nidal Saadeh

ISBN: 153989360X

ISBN 13: 9781539893608

Disclaimer

Although the author and publisher have made every effort to ensure that the information in this book was correct at press time, the author and publisher do not assume and hereby disclaim any liability to any party for any loss, damage, or disruption caused by errors or omissions, whether such errors or omissions result from negligence, accident, or any other cause.

This book (refer to the chapter on "How to Heal Oneself via the Force") is not intended as a substitute for the medical advice of physicians. The reader should regularly consult a physician in matters relating to his or her health and particularly with respect to any symptoms that may require diagnosis or medical attention.

The information contained within this book is strictly for educational purposes. If you wish to apply ideas contained in this book, you are taking full responsibility for your actions. The author and the publisher make no guarantees that the reader will achieve the same results.

To my beautiful children, may God bless them always.

Contents

Preface

In writing this book, I have tried to convey to the reader a simple way of understanding and performing the practical exercises laid out throughout the book in order to improve and achieve success in any area of their life, including optimal health, material wealth, total happiness, and any other personal desires or goals.

I have spent many years in senior-management roles within large companies around the world and set up and run my own businesses to this day with amazing results; therefore, with the many hundreds of employees I have employed, trained, and managed throughout my working life, I have had the pleasure of changing the lives of many with respect to personal development, personal achievement, and personal growth. After many years of contemplating my own personal achievements and the achievements of others I've looked up to, I found myself on a journey to discover how events have transpired in my life and the lives of others.

It all started when studying and researching many self-help and personal-development pioneers of the past and present. It was when I read the books *The Science of Getting Rich* by Wallace D. Wattles and the famous book *Think and Grow Rich* by Napoleon Hill several times that I became extremely fascinated by the way personal development could be achieved through new thought, metaphysics, and the concept of creative thinking. After exploring many more authors and speakers from the late eighteen hundreds and early nineteen hundreds, I discovered that a lot of my beliefs were the root cause of my life's attractions and achievements, which led me to source more information to satisfy my need for more answers on how life happens to us and how we can be deliberate creators. As I delved deeper and deeper into the knowledge of new thought and metaphysics, I found that there were many ways in which authors and speakers delivered the same message, and at times I became somewhat confused by all the metaphors, scriptural language, and the lack of understanding of how I could actually use this knowledge in a practical way for my benefit. But still I remained somewhat committed to finding out more about the subject matter. After much inspiration from my findings from all my mentors, and applying my own thoughts and creative ideas to a process which I have used time and time again and shared with many people over the years who have achieved great results, I decided to write this book to inspire and help change the lives of others.

In writing this book, I have tried to keep the readers engaged, intrigued, eager, and motivated to gain an understanding of how to implement the knowledge shared in this book for the benefit of self-development and personal achievement in all areas of their lives. I have kept each chapter clear, concise, and consistent for complete comprehension of how to prepare one's mind and use the creative process to achieve all that is desired, by anyone who reads my book. I've included success stories of many individuals I've shared my knowledge with, not to mention some personal accounts of my own results using the knowledge laid down herein as proof it works. My hope is you find this book resourceful, interesting, and fruitful.

Nidal Saadeh

Introduction

There are some things that happen to us in our lives that we never want to accept, and we find ourselves asking many questions. Why did this happen to me? What did I do to deserve this? Why don't things work out for me the way I want them to? And then we are constantly looking for answers. We never want to accept that it's our fault deep down. It's always someone else's. It was going to happen anyway. It was fate or just bad luck. Well, after extensive research, I have come to believe there has to be some major Force beyond our comprehension running the show, a Force that works with us, for us, and through us, and we can direct this Force through our imagination to live life by design and not by chance.

As a person with an analytical mind, I have always been very curious about how things happen to us in life, perhaps as much as the next person. I wonder how my life has turned out the way it has for me thus far.

After endless studying and researching several books on self-help, mind power, new thought, spiritual science, religion, quantum physics, metaphysics, and much more over the past ten years, I have come to the understanding and conclusion that we are responsible for everything that happens in our lives—I mean everything.

Here is a case study of someone I have mentored who, like many, at first did not believe that we are responsible for what happens in our lives. He believed he was just unfortunate all the time, that the whole world was against him, and that he was a victim of circumstances. Well, he went from job to job with a total of eight jobs in four years, and it was the same old story every time: "My boss is not very nice. He treats me badly. My colleagues are antisocial and are given more privileges…" You get the picture. He believed he was always right and did nothing wrong; everything was someone else's fault, and he had to get away to the next job because he believed it was going to be better. This would happen time and time again. Incidentally, I've helped him over the years, and he is doing very well in life now, enjoying stability, great health, and abundance and doing what he loves best, working in the medical field, providing specialist equipment for the elderly and people with disabilities. He was a difficult case to convince, as he suffers from bipolar disorder, a mental illness that makes him manic in his behavior. I helped him manage it, so to speak.

Well, I decided to write this book to help and share with as many people in the world as possible information on how you can have, be, and do anything you want in life, regardless of your health, background, education, or financial status. My ultimate goal for writing this book is that anyone who reads it will, with practice, master the art of creative thinking to achieve his or her every desire and goals for a better life. You will need to have an open mind while reading this book, as it may be hard to accept the information at first. You may find it all very new to you indeed. It may even seem unbelievable and all too good to be true, but I do urge you to try it and see for yourself.

As for myself, well, I am not going to give you a sob story and say that I was broke, down on my luck, homeless, had no education, and came from a poor family; that's not my story. However, this information, over time, has created some rags-to-riches stories for sure. I have heard examples from past students of mine, in addition to other stories from authors and speakers I am familiar with. However, I do believe that how you were raised and programmed by your environment when you were young plays a big part in what happens to you, what you achieve, and what you get in life.

I was raised well by my parents, who were quite ambitious in their early days, especially my father. They did their very best to give me a comfortable start in life, not to mention a good education. Like most parents of the sixties and seventies, my parents told me time and time again to study hard, get out there, and get a good job with a big company to do well in life.

For well over ten years, I've been obsessed with why certain things have happened to me in my life, good and bad, and have conducted research through books and the Internet. I have always believed that there is some kind of Force—call it what you will—an unseen Force, an invisible power that creates our lives as we go along, and some people know how to deliberately work this Force to their advantage, while others do just by accident. Many would see these people as lucky for all the good fortune they have that gives them abundant, healthy, and blissful lives. This invisible Force is constant; it's active all the time, whether we acknowledge it, try to comprehend it, or even refuse to believe in it. We know and take for granted magnetic forces, electrical forces, and the force of gravity, yet we can't see these forces. They are invisible to the naked eye, but we know from science that they exist, because we utilize and direct these forces for useful purposes in our daily lives. These forces, however, have been around since the start of time, and they remained undiscovered for many years. I believe there is an invisible Force like many other forces in this universe today. We are part of this Force; we are not separate from it. It guides us through our intuition, it controls and runs our bodies' systems throughout our waking lives, and (last but not least) it heals us when we are ill.

This Force creates our lives through our constant thinking, our different states of mind, and our imagination. So, control your thoughts, and you control how your life unfolds. I explain how you can do this with a practical exercise laid out in this book. So continue to read and be intrigued.

Everything you can imagine is real.

—Pablo Picasso

Chapter One

How I Came to Know the Power of the Force

Like I said, I have always had a fascination for finding out why things have turned out like they have for me thus far, and I asked myself if there was a formula, or if it was fate, luck, just meant to be, or all a coincidence?

Well, now I really do get it—big time. I truly understand why and how things happen to us, and I want to share my knowledge with you in a very simple-to-understand format so you can take it in, internalize it, and use it for the fulfillment of a better life. It may be that you want better health, new love, the perfect job or business, financial wealth, a dream vacation, or a life with all your wishes and desires fulfilled. I have been inspired to write this book by what I have learned from all the philosophies I have read and heard and my own personal account of good fortune from my own experiences in life. I have not used any analogies, metaphors, or scriptural language in this book, as I wish to convey a clear and simple message to the reader and avoid any confusion.

I have realized that whatever has happened to me in life for good or bad was no accident. I was the cause of it all—yes, all of it, good and bad. I still sometimes catch myself thinking otherwise, and then I quickly correct myself, knowing what I know now.

Let me describe the process in simple terms without a detailed scientific explanation. We are all energy; everything in the universe is energy. We are all one, all connected. Energy, as we know from science, is neither created nor destroyed. It changes forms all the time. All forces of nature are energy. All things in our reality are made of energy. Everything is vibrating at various frequencies. The thoughts we think are energy; so as we think our thoughts and as we entertain our thoughts in our minds, whatever they may be, we create our feelings, which are vibrations of energy. So the thought energy we emit via the Force is vibrating at a certain frequency. This energy is part of the invisible Force that brings into our reality the objective fact of whatever it may be we were imagining and sensing in our thoughts. Our thoughts influence our reality and the experiences we have in life.

You see, your life is a true reflection of your accumulated past thoughts. Everything that is in your reality in this universe came to pass out of your preceding thoughts.

> Imagination is everything. It is the preview of life's coming attractions.

> —Albert Einstein

When I got to grips with this amazing discovery, I decided that I wanted to go back in time and try to remember moments in my life when I received material wealth, which I always desired, and opportunities that led me to achieving my goals and a life of abundance. I learned that I was operating this Force in a positive way by default at certain times in my life and didn't know it. I discovered it from many mentors and spiritual teachers I have been studying over the past few years.

I would think to myself, "This is truly amazing. I have the golden recipe for life; it's like having a formula to win the lotto over and over again." I used to look around at other people, knowing most were ignorant of this fact. I felt very privileged to know this information but wanted to share it with everyone I came into contact with. It was like a duty to do so, giving something back to the universe as a thank-you.

I grew up, like most people, thinking I had to work hard in life because that was what I was taught. I always had a positive attitude and wanted to do my best in all I did. But in the beginning, it didn't help. I never got what I really wanted, and nothing seemed to work out for me. It seemed to work for others who didn't appear to work that hard at all. It kind of made me envy them somewhat but in a good way.

I liked my first occupation in life just after finishing college, but I didn't really like the environment. It was destructive, and employees were negative toward one another. Knowing what I know now, I recognize it was me, my creation entirely. You may ask why. Continue reading and you will understand why I take responsibility for all my experiences in life—all of them without fail.

I want to explain the whole picture so you fully understand this powerful knowledge for yourself and can utilize it to obtain an abundant life, like so many in this world are experiencing today, because after all, we were never born to struggle.

Anyway, one day, I thought about quitting my job, just like that. I thought there must be something better out there for me. This couldn't be it. I didn't want to spend the next thirty to forty years doing the same old thing, day in and day out. I needed to change my life completely. I was in my early twenties, and I had an urge to change course in life for something better with better prospects, so I thought about driving to southern Spain to start a new life. Everyone at the time thought I was mad, leaving a great job, family, and friends for a life unknown. I had no idea what I was going to do when I reached Spain. I just felt that was where I wanted to be. I had vacationed in Spain with friends and would dream constantly of driving there and parking outside my usual restaurant where I had spent good times with my friends. I would visualize myself driving down the long country roads through Spain, waving to Spanish farmers along the way, shouting hello in Spanish. I would imagine the warm weather and the air rushing past my hand as I held it out of my car window.

I spent many days and nights dreaming I was in Spain, living and working there, driving to my favorite locations, meeting up with my friends whom I'd met on my previous trips, and after a couple of weeks, I actually felt as if I were already there in my imagination.

About three weeks later, everything seemed to happen naturally, and the events that unfolded made me quit and head for Spain. I have to say it was a big decision to leave a good career that I had studied four years at college for. No one had really ever quit a job with the firm I was with, because it was considered a job for life. The events that led up to it were bizarre, and with all my experiences in life, it would seem that it was all my physical effort that brought everything to fruition—but no, it was this Force in action, creating from my thoughts and feelings the whole dream into an objective fact. The events leading up to my move included my parents deciding to live in Spain out of the blue. They sold their dream home in England, which they had never discussed or planned on doing. My sister called me up saying she was in Spain with a new job. All this happened within weeks. It was about three months later when I was in Spain that I remembered my dreams, and as I was sitting in my usual bar, looking out and seeing my car parked outside, I told myself, "Wow, it's a dream come true." Now, you may be thinking, "Well, you made it happen anyway." Yes, I made a decision and took action, but everything seemed to happen with ease and my plans just fell into place. I was encouraged and influenced by the events that led up to the whole event, making my move very natural. You see, if these events had not happened, I probably wouldn't have made the decision to leave.

Events happened the same way with my other amazing experiences later on in life, which I will share with you throughout this book. It turned out to be the best move I ever made and the start of a journey that brought wealth, health, and happiness, not only for me but for my family too. You see, when you use the Force correctly, it will amaze you all the time how things show up and materialize for you. Events you least expect to happen will happen to get you what you want or where you want go in life.

Thoughts and feelings become our reality, our life experiences. I didn't know this before; I always thought things just happened to me for a reason. It was my destiny or just fate.

All that we are is a result of what we have thought.

—Buddha

Later in life, I would imagine myself doing well at whatever I set my mind on, and the results were phenomenal. I saw myself working in senior-management roles in corporate companies all over the world, earning more money than I ever thought was possible from what I was used to doing. It all became surreal for me. In my first company, within six months of arriving in Spain, I took my annual income to a monthly income, and within three to four years, I took it much higher. It continued to grow. I didn't know why this had happened then. I just put it down to a positive personality, ability to do the job, hard work, and many long hours. It was the invisible Force in action, I know now. I share the formula with you throughout this book.

You may find yourself reading this book over and over to really grasp the concept and the art of creating via the Force.

Looking back, I see that everything I imagined appeared in my life. I would see myself settled down with children, and it became so. I would visualize buying property and living in a grand detached home with large gardens, and it became true. I achieved financial independence at an early age. I would also see myself with an athletic body, and now I am much fitter, healthier, and in good shape. Knowing what I know now, I created all that from imagining in a certain way via the Force.

I looked at my father's life and realized he was and still is a natural at using this Force in his life to become, do, or have whatever he imagines. He did this by default, as he was none the wiser. Let me give you an example. Father lived in a small town in the Middle East. When he was seventeen, he would watch British war planes fly through the sky over his small town. He told me he would then see himself flying in his imagination, literally sitting in the cockpit and experiencing all the feelings of flying. Later in life, he managed to cross the border to Amman, Jordan, and out of fifty applicants, he was one of the six accepted into the Royal Jordanian Air Force. He became a first-class pilot and won many awards flying in the British Royal Air Force in the United Kingdom. He also visualized himself flying for the late King Hussein to impress his parents, and not long after, he was called up to see the late king of Jordan and was assigned to be his private pilot as part of his protocol in the Royal Jordanian Air Force.

His dreams came true. His thoughts and feelings from his imagination created his reality. You see, it's not an accident; he was using the Force to his advantage by default until I shared this knowledge with him. You will learn to do so as you read through this book.

A man is but the product of his thoughts. What he thinks
he becomes.

—Gandhi

All that is desired can be imagined into existence.

—Neville Goddard

Readers notes

Chapter Two

The Force

There are many forces in the universe, but all emanate from one Force, which creates everything in existence. I believe if you look at what's around us in nature, you will see an abundance of life in action, created via the Force.

Everything flows without any restrictions. There is a large willow tree in my garden, and it always amazes me how when I have it cut, cropped, and generally pruned, it grows back tenfold in abundance. That in itself reminds me, there is no limit in life to what we can have or experience. There is enough to go around for everyone on our planet. It's infinite.

The Force I refer to may be called by many as infinite intelligence, source energy, God, Allah (God in Arabic), our higher self, spiritual energy, Mother Nature, and many other names for the creator of all things. Many people don't understand that we are all one, and we cocreate our lives with this Force. They think we are all separate, life just happens to us, it's mapped out for each of us, and we have no control.

We humans have been gifted with a mind to think and attract into our lives anything we want, but many people allow circumstances to dictate their lives. They sail through life, hoping for the best and looking forward to good things just showing up in their lives by chance. It doesn't have to be that way at all. Once you know how to use the Force for a perfect life, you will want to use it to your advantage forever.

The thoughts we think create our feelings. If our thoughts are positive, we enter a state of mind in which we feel upbeat, and it appears so in our experiences in life. If we think negative thoughts, we enter a state of mind where we feel low, and these negative thoughts manifest in our experiences in life. Let's go into detail here for a minute, as we know everything is energy. Our body is energy. We broadcast positive waves of energy when we think positive thoughts. Our feelings create a high frequency, and when this frequency tunes in to exactly the same frequencies via the Force, we receive these waves of energy back in the form of our physical reality. For example, positive people will show up in our lives, unexpected e-mails appear, and phone calls come out of the blue, as do new situations, plans for travel, opportunities, and relationships—basically, we experience a complete change of circumstances, and events and experiences appear.

This is the Force in action. Nothing stops it. It is constant and is always in motion. When we have negative thoughts, we broadcast negative waves of energy in the form of low frequencies, which tune in to similar frequencies. They are perfectly tuned, and we receive these waves back in the form of our reality, but in this case, negative people will generally show up in our lives, and bad situations will occur, for example, money issues, poor health, lack of opportunities, negative relationships, depression, and unexpected problems—the complete opposite of happiness, prosperity, joy, and bliss in life. It's quite clear what I decided to do to better my life. I decided to keep my thoughts positive at all times.

You may say it's hard to be happy and maintain positive thoughts all the time. Well, you see, it's like going to the gym to exercise. Not many like to go and work out; it's too much like hard work. It's tedious and somewhat boring, to say the least. I know this because I have forced myself to go five days a week for the past twenty-odd years. However when you go, get started, and keep it up, each time, it gets better and easier. When the results start to show, you become addicted, and you can't stop going. You become programmed, just like the muscles in your body get programmed. We call it muscle memory; it just tones right back up there as soon as we start to pump iron during our workout. It's like that for the mind too. When you start to focus on your thoughts and keep them only on positive things, it will become a habit, and it will be an easy thing to do over time. Eventually, your mind will block nearly all negative thoughts on autopilot through your awareness. There will be times when you react to a situation or person that catches you off guard; it happens to me from time to time. It's normal. When it does, just reflect on your past moods, thoughts, and behavior, and you will then recognize why negative events or people have suddenly appeared in your life. Be conscious of them to prevent further negative encounters.

You see, the mind is everything—if only we would use it properly. You just have to get it started and practice the art of thinking positive things all the time, and it will get easier with time for sure. By the way, I am preparing your mind for what comes next, as it is critical to the creative process to have a positive-thinking mind.

Once you establish this habitual way of thinking, you will find your life will begin to change drastically. The way you feel will change. The people you want to hang around with or draw to you will be of a happy, positive, and prosperous nature. You will attract into your life many positive events, new relationships, better job opportunities with more money, and material wealth. Your business will start to flourish and expand beyond your comprehension. You will start to see things you didn't see before around you and also start to appreciate things around you, such as nature in its entirety. I know this for a fact, as I make time in my life to observe the birds, the trees in my gardens, and all of nature's animals. Time will begin to expand. You will feel you have more time on your hands than ever before. You see, when we focus on the fact that we are busy and have no time and get wrapped up in negative situations, that's what appears in our lives via the Force: the feeling of running out of time and experiencing constant issues and problems. Remember this, you may have heard it before, but it's a good quote to know: "Where your focus goes, your energy flows." Whatever you put your mind on and believe it to be fact or true, it will appear in your life. The mind does not know the difference between imagined acts and acts carried out in the physical world. Science has proven this fact with tests on the human brain.

Some people don't realize this and continue to entertain negative thinking as it becomes the norm in their minds to do so. They constantly feel bad. They complain all the time. They moan of ill health, gossip constantly, and gloat over others' misfortunes. This is a cycle of constant negative thinking and a recipe for disaster, a life of misery, poverty, bad luck, ill health, and unhappiness, but they continue to do it. Why? Because they don't know any better. It's how they were programmed at an early age in life. Your mental programs become your fixed, limiting beliefs that control how you think, your thoughts of others, your beliefs about money, your self-image, your communication skills, your behavior, and your self-belief in life as you get older. It's like your mental hard drive is playing on a loop. You see, beliefs are nothing more than thought repetition in the subconscious mind that shapes your future.

I mentioned earlier in this book that I believe programming plays a big part in what we receive in life as a result of our thoughts and feelings. The programs in our subconscious mind limit us to the life we lead, the reason being, from the moment of conception to about the age of seven, our minds are wide open and take in everything we see, hear, feel, and sense. You may have heard the expression "A child's mind is like a sponge." Well, our young mind receives information from the environment from all kinds of influences, for example, parents, grandparents, other relatives, schoolteachers, friends, television, what we hear on the radio, what we see in nature, and what we experience in our day-to-day lives. Our senses interpret and store the information, and this becomes our programs, our limiting beliefs, our habits, and our habitual way of thinking in life, which we act out in our adult life as our fundamental coping skills.

Some of these programs we didn't ask for, by the way, and they don't always work to our advantage in life. We just happened to be there, taking them all in when we were infants and children. These programs don't serve us for many reasons. Let's take the subject of money, for example. Many of us grew up feeling bad about money. It was like a dirty word. We were told it's the root of all evil, or we grew up where our parents didn't really have enough money and were constantly talking about it in a negative way. There was that feeling of scarcity in the family from arguments about bills and comments like "We can't afford this and can't afford that." Our young mind, whether we recall it or not, picked this up, and it became a limiting belief, which was fixed in our mind and made us believe in our adulthood we can only earn or have a certain amount of money and we are not worthy of being wealthy in life. We watch what we spend; we become frugal and feel guilty if we buy something expensive, because we came from an upbringing of lack. This limiting belief is thought energy that will only produce a low frequency being emitted via the Force. Therefore, it creates more scarcity and lack in life.

By the way, it's not uncommon to hear of people becoming successful and wealthy in life even though they came from a family background of lack. They have mastered the art of thinking in a certain way and carry beliefs quite different from their family members'. They have believed in themselves and had big dreams in life with unwavering faith.

People who were raised in a family with money and material wealth, who always talked about money in a positive way, never negatively, tend to spend money in a frivolous way in their adult life without worrying it's going to run out. They seem to have all the finer things in life, such as all the latest modern conveniences you may find on display in the stores. They live in luxury homes and drive expensive cars; they constantly travel first class to exotic destinations and stay in quality hotels or other homes they own, as there seems to be no limit to what they spend, have, or do in life. They also seem to be ambitious and follow the footsteps of their parents with high-flying careers or become entrepreneurs.

So if you grew up in that environment, you will have a belief of prosperity, a program that there is plenty of money, never any shortage, and there is enough to go around for everyone to enjoy. With this mind-set, you believe you can have more in life and you get more, whatever it may be. This mind-set carries a vibration that is a high frequency of positive energy. It's a frequency that does not contain the vibration of worry, fear, or doubt, which, by the way, is the frequency that creates a life of lack, poverty, misery, and not to mention poor health. Fear, doubt, and worry block us from living a life of freedom. For example, fear prevents us from changing jobs, moving, asking someone out on a date, public speaking, singing, flying, going on a boat, and so on. It's a negative belief held in the mind that keeps us stuck in life and kills all desires.

This goes for everything in life. If your beliefs are of a positive nature, you can expect to have sound physical health, financial wealth, happiness, freedom, and joy, which all human beings strive to have in life. It's your limiting beliefs, your habitual way of thinking, that holds you back from having everything you desire from life.

People have asked me, "OK, that's all well and good. If we have limiting beliefs from our programming, what can we do about it? Are we stuck with these programs? How do we reprogram or erase these limiting beliefs from our subconscious mind so we can achieve more in life?"

Well, I discovered for myself that you can reprogram yourself in many ways: one being hypnosis, either self or by a qualified therapist. I've successfully reprogrammed myself with NLP (neurolinguistic programming), which I have studied. I completed a master-practitioner course, which has proven very useful for me and my students. I have used this technique along with EFT (emotional freedom technique), a very powerful technique, and it is a fast way to reprogram your mind.

OK, let's take EFT for this exercise. I am not going to explain EFT in this book, because there is an untold amount of EFT information and tutorial videos on the Internet that will guide you on how to use it successfully. Don't be alarmed. It's not complicated; it's very easy to use and very effective.

EFT is a very fast and effective way to remove limiting beliefs from the mind. It is also used to remove emotional issues. It is performed by way of tapping on meridian locations around the head and body with our fingers. As we do this, we are tapping for specific beliefs that limit us from getting ahead in life.

When I first used this technique, I personally sat down and recalled memories of a negative nature, memories I felt did not serve me, and, of course, beliefs that I knew were holding me back and hampering my chances of future success. I focused on each event in my mind and made them so vivid it felt as if I were experiencing the events all over again in the present. When I would start to feel the sensations in my body of a specific memory, I would tap out the issues from this memory in my mind while verbalizing the correct EFT language on the topic matter until I would feel it was no longer there in the mind. I would aim to neutralize it on a rating from zero to ten, ten being blocked and zero being cleared. How did I know it was at zero? Well, I would feel very light-headed and totally relaxed. I would experience a sense of relief and also would have some difficulty trying to recall the memory the way it happened. It appeared different. My perception of it had changed, and it felt different when I came out from that state of mind. It didn't bother or affect me anymore. For some cases, it would take more than one session of EFT to clear the blockage from the belief, because there would be more than one event that happened, feeding that memory or belief, but it works wonders. We call this *reframing* in NLP (neurolinguistic programming). It's a way of changing an experience, so your response to that experience changes.

Negative memories of any nature, for example, the loss of a loved one, a painful divorce, or any kind of relationship breakdown in which someone has injured or hurt you badly, carry negative energy, and they continue to emit negative frequencies via the Force on a subconscious level and match and attract similar frequencies via the Force, which show up in our reality in a negative way. So when you neutralize these memories, you cancel out the potential of this happening. You see, some people have many relationships in life that don't work out, and they can't understand why. Well, it's all programming. They may have had parents who divorced or parents who had many unstable relationships themselves, and this has been their programming from a young age. It later plays out in their lives, causing their relationships to be dysfunctional as well. When you change the belief, you change the energy of your thoughts and feelings emitted as a frequency via the Force, thus changing the habit and the experiences in your life.

Negative memories, we know, exist in various ways. Some are visual and some auditory. They can be triggered by anchors, for example, a tune or song on the radio, a photograph, a movie, or seeing someone who reminds you of a specific memory. Some memories are nonvisual, but you know they are there. They express themselves in your body through hurt or pain. You feel them in the body from time to time so you know they're from something that happened to you. You can't recall the experiences visually, but there is a link. These types of memories carry a negative energy that makes you think and feel negatively, which affects the quality of your life.

When memories are triggered, you feel the emotions throughout your body, and you feel the same sensations, as if the experience were happening to you again in the present moment in time. The body reacts in the same way every time the memories are triggered. It doesn't know the difference between past and present. It believes it's in the same environment. The fight-or-flight response activates, and you feel the fear, hurt, and pain once again. These feelings emit a negative frequency via the Force and create more of the same events, situations, and circumstances in your reality. So I believed, by reprogramming my negative memories or clearing them, I would only have positive memories and beliefs in my subconscious, which would affect my experiences in reality in a positive way.

Once we have neutralized or cleared our negative memories and reprogrammed our limiting beliefs on whatever it may have been that was holding us back in life and blocking our minds in some way or another, life will start to change. Our attitude from our reprogramming will alter, and we will feel totally different. Then we can practice what I call "rehearsal of the past," a process to mentally change the outcome of past events. This practice is very effective and raises our vibration effectively. Anyone can do this.

I would recall any experience in my life that didn't turn out the way I wanted it to and rehearse the whole episode in my mind so that it would. You see, I believe you can change the story of any past event in your imagination, as all past memories are energy. They can be changed to appear positive and carry with them the positive feelings and sensations in your body as though the story has changed for the better with the desired outcome. By doing this, you change the vibration of the energy and the frequency from these thoughts and feelings you are emitting via the Force; therefore, you enable yourself to reap the benefits in your reality. If these past episodes are left unrehearsed, they remain alive in the subconscious and continue to contribute to the overall energy sphere around your body, emitting a negative frequency via the Force and causing adversity to appear in one's life over and over again. It is very important to carry out this process. When you rehearse the undesired past events, you affect and change what will appear in your life in the present and the future. This is all done by the powerful Force, which is energy. Remember, energy can't be destroyed, can't be created, is always in motion, and is always actively creating.

This Force, when infused with your thoughts and feelings, which is your vibration either high or low, will display a true reflection on what I call your screen of life, your physical reality. Everything you want or do not want is in the Force. We only receive in life a perfect replica of the exact frequency we are broadcasting via the Force from our thoughts and feelings.

Now that you know how to clear up your mind and your energy field and focus on positive thinking, I can share with you the creative process.

> To bring anything into your life, imagine that it's already there.
>
> —Richard Bach

> Your worst enemy cannot harm you as much as your own unguarded thoughts.
>
> —Buddha

Readers notes

Chapter Three

How to Rehearse the Past

Let me explain a practical way of rehearsing past events to change negative experiences into positive ones that will influence your present and future reality. For example, you can revisit in your imagination, a time, place, or situation when you may have been, hurt, injured, mistreated, abandoned, or rejected. This may be from an ex-partner, an old teacher, a former employer, a friend, a family member, or anyone in an episode that was a negative experience in your life. You can change it to alter the outcome.

Find a place where you can have some quiet time and privacy with no disturbance for at least ten to fifteen minutes. You may wish to do this before you sleep at night; it's highly effective. By the way, I have used this process to change any episode in my life, old or new, and continue to do so with great success. OK, let's continue. Bring a past event into your mind's eye. You need to put yourself in the episode. Play it out in your mind like you are in the movie. You are not the observer of yourself in the movie; you are in the movie as you. Act out the whole episode as it happened, but instead of the existing ending, change the scene to your desired ending. During this process, feel all the sensations from the background noises. See what you saw, feel how you felt at the time, and hear what you heard. Add as much detail as possible to enhance the feeling of realism. It's normal to get upset during the session, especially if it's a painful experience you are recalling, but if you do, it's a sign you are doing it right.

If you are in conversation with someone who upset you for whatever reason, see and hear his or her responses. See the person being nice to you and smiling. Feel the grip of his or her warm handshake or the embrace of a genuine hug, and experience total understanding of the subject matter, giving the whole story a new meaning, with a feel-good factor all throughout your movie. During this time, you will be in what I call a controlled daydream—or you could call it a controlled state of mind. If you do the process right, you will feel totally aroused and emotionally charged from all your senses. You will experience total abandonment of yourself during the process and a feeling of being not present elsewhere; you will be back in that moment, reliving that whole episode again.

Do this process several times until it feels completely real, and you believe and feel it has changed; then watch how the Force brings about change and how your screen of life begins to display positive events with different feelings and experiences. If it's a current situation you wish to change, maybe an unhappy relationship with your partner in business, wife or husband, friend, family member, or current employer, use this process.

Run through the process outlined above and imagine it with all the feelings and all senses of reality, and play the whole scene differently. See your wife, husband, or partner responding with love and affection. See a friend being amicable and gracious with you, the boss singing your praise and giving you a pat on the back or a raise in pay. Feel the positive responses as if they were real. Follow the process to the letter, and you will be amazed how things will appear on your screen of life. In the following days and weeks to come, your reality will feel different. Most people try to change what's on their screen, the physical world, and it always fails. It's the changes on the inside in our minds that project a different story and picture on the outside. This process is ideal if you want to rehearse the receipt of bad news, be it via a phone call, letter, e-mail, or face to face. The news may be, for example, not getting the job you applied for or that your home didn't sell. Change the desired outcome in your controlled daydream sessions to the point it feels changed to you, and it will be so if you remain true to your desired outcome and allow nothing to interfere or affect it.

Remember, you need to put yourself in the episode as you and play it out in your mind as though you are in your own movie. You are not the observer of yourself in the movie. You are in the movie as you. This is very important if you want to see perfect results.

> What you radiate outward in your thoughts, feelings, men-
> tal pictures, and words, you attract into your life.
>
> —Catherine Ponder

> Whatever you create in your life you must first create in
> your imagination.
>
> —Tycho Photiou

This process is good to perform at the end of each day before you retire to sleep if you wish to change the outcome of any event to your liking that day. It will change how events and experiences turn out for you in the coming days or weeks ahead. If you leave it alone, you can expect more of the same, so rehearse the past for a better future.

Readers notes

Chapter Four

Creating via the Force

What is most important is to know what you really want out of life. When you know what it is you want to have, be, or do in life, you can create the whole movie in your mind's eye with all the feelings and senses you would experience if it were happening for real. Remember, you are creating your own script in your own movie as yourself, acting out all the things you would do as if it were real and in the present tense. You will begin to experience a whole new episode in your reality in the days, weeks, or maybe months that follow. There will be evidence of your desire unfolding, and as the signs and uncanny happenings appear in your day-to-day life, you will feel elated and amazed; it will feel like it's a natural occurrence at times, that it was going to take place anyway and your physical acts were the cause, but no, it is the Force in action, providing you with a true reflection of your thoughts and feelings from your mental movie. As you gaze with amazement and disbelief, you will become aroused and excited, and your vibration will increase, therefore contributing to a higher frequency, emitting from your body's sphere of energy. Then more amazing things will appear on your screen of life (physical world). You will feel very powerful; indeed, you won't be able to contain yourself. You will want to share this wisdom with everyone you know. Some won't believe you. They will give credit to the events and actions that preceded the outcome, but that's OK. You will know it's the Force in action and will continue to create more experiences through it.

After learning of this Force, I realized that the past events in my life were not a coincidence. I had created my past via the Force, which, by the way, has been used by many people over the centuries. It was left in scripture and passed down through the ages for us all to understand and use in our daily lives to fulfill all our dreams and desires.

I had practiced the knowledge by default, but like I mentioned earlier, I didn't know it then. I wasn't aware of the Force. My beliefs were different back then. Here is an example of how I achieved one of the many desires that materialized in my life. I was in my late teens, and what was on my mind, like most teenagers of that age, was to buy and drive a sporty car. Well, there was a car out on the market at that time, and it was a very sought-after car. It really stood out, but unfortunately, it was well out of my financial reach.

I thought at the time, "I will own one, one day." Well, I became fixated on this car, reading up on it and watching reviews on motor shows on TV, but what I did next really was truly amazing. I used to spend a lot of time up in my bedroom, listening to my favorite music, like most teenagers do even today, but while I was listening to the music, I would imagine driving this car as if it were mine around town. I would see the sceneries as I would see in reality, I would hear the purr of the engine, and I could smell the new-ness of the interior. I would have the stereo up loud, and the music in my room would actually contribute to my daydream. I also played around with switches in the car, and I could hear the great sound of the exhaust system. I got into a state of mind where I felt I was no longer in my room. I was in my new sports car. I was feeling all the sensations in my mind and body of the excitement and all the senses of reality. I would see people on the sidewalk, looking at me in this car. I would park and hear my friends and strangers passing by, commenting on my new car in amazement.

I remember doing this whole controlled daydream session for many weeks. I can't remember how many, but it was just over a month. It wasn't planned either; I would do it naturally for the feeling of what it would be like. Then one day, I was passing by my father's friend's used-car showroom, and I saw the car I wanted, but in the color blue. The one I was imagining was black. Anyway, I spoke to him and he advised me the car had just arrived and was being prepared for sale. By the way, the price tag was still out of my reach by a thousand pounds, and I didn't want to borrow the money. I wasn't a fan of debt. I was programmed to always save up and pay cash for everything, and if I could not afford it, I didn't buy it. That didn't stop me sitting in the car, playing with the electric windows, getting familiar with the whole feel of the car. It was a perfect opportunity to do so. As you read through this book, you will realize this event was no accident; it was the Force in action.

The sales manager said to me, "Have you driven a car like this before?"

I said, "No, not yet, but I would like to." Before I knew it, he kindly let me test-drive it for an hour, one whole hour. I remember being elated. I was very excited and motivated. I could hardly believe my luck. I went everywhere in it, all around town. It was a perfect match to my controlled daydreams, to what I had imagined. I had the radio on, the music turned up, and the AC on, and I was in heaven for a young man of eighteen. People turned around to watch the car drive by. It was a teenager's dream come true. Well, I returned the car, and it made me more determined to own this type of car, even though I could not afford it. I felt I could in my mind. I continued to imagine driving the car in a controlled daydream while listening to music in my room for weeks after. I remember they became more vivid as I had the true feelings from the test drive now to reflect on, and as I did, it was even more real in my mind than it ever felt before. Two weeks later, I was called into the head office at work and was given longer hours and more pay for a new contract. I was very happy indeed, as this was what would finally get me this car.

I worked a couple of months, but saving was harder than I thought, as I had living expenses and college fees to cover. Then one weekend, my mother, who didn't know much about cars, out of the blue spotted this car in the color black in the local newspaper. I couldn't believe my eyes. It was well underpriced. I thought there might have been something wrong with it, and if not, surely it was sold by then. I jumped on the phone. To my amazement, it was still available, and the man was in a rush to sell because of the arrival of a new baby. He did not need such a car, as it wasn't practical. I raced up to his home and privately bought the car, and it was well within my financial means. I drove back, feeling quite surreal at how I had managed to get the car of my desire. I could not get my head around it for days thereafter. I thought it must have been fate or pure luck at that time. It was the Force creating and manifesting my desire in its entirety. It didn't happen all at once, but the sequence of events led up to the goal of getting my dream car for a price well under the market value.

You see, my thoughts and feelings created the exact frequency that was perfectly tuned to what finally appeared in my reality. Remember, you get back from the Force exactly what you imagine with emotionalized thinking. The whole episode was a true reflection of my thoughts and feelings. As I felt the episode to be true to me, it became a fact, fulfilled, and a done deal in the mind, so it had to appear on my screen of life, known to all of us as our physical reality.

This creative process now known to me is what I call a controlled daydream. It is what I have been using for the fulfillment of all my desires, needs, and goals in life to this day.

I have used this whole creative process for obtaining great opportunities and major achievements in business, as I previously mentioned, for example, seeing myself in senior positions in large companies in different countries all over of the world with great income, running my own successful businesses, having financial independence, owning several properties, and much more.

One particular opportunity stands out. I wanted to work for a particular firm again and earn a big income. I would envisage myself as already in a director role, conducting large meetings and going about business in a corporate way. This whole episode would be conducted in a controlled daydream with all the sensory conditions, the sounds I would hear, the people I would meet, the atmosphere I would feel, as though it were totally real and happening in the present tense. I would put myself in that country, feeling and seeing all the things I would see and feel as if I were there, looking back at where I was in my old location. It was a few months later that I was working for a large firm, as a company director, earning more money than I even imagined in my creative process. It was extraordinary, and it felt like I had hit the jackpot. Of course, action is always necessary once your desire presents itself in reality; for example, you must have the ability to take on the role and undertake the training you have to have to master your craft and improve your skills. You have to have the ability to carry out your desire once in the role for real. Talent comes from intense practice. A pilot can't be a pilot unless he or she trains to be, and a doctor can't be a doctor unless he or she studies medicine. It's about visualizing yourself getting the opportunity and playing out the role in your mind's eye—you with the fulfilled desire—is what I'm trying to convey. Creative thought without action is futile.

I was always amazed how things panned out for me and really became obsessed with using the process not only to create but to change current situations for a better experience and positive outcome of future events in my life, for example, meetings, interviews, and social events. It was astounding how I could create the desired outcomes of behaviors of others and even the results, all through the creative process.

I have shared this information on a day-to-day basis and continue to do so wherever I go and with the many people I meet, especially family members, friends, and students. I have had such great feedback; it always amazes me as much as the people telling me about their changed situation, whether it's a new job, a new relationship, or a better relationship with a boss, spouse, neighbor, or whatever it may be. It's funny, but they never refer back to the process. They talk about their new encounter as if they just had a change of luck and everything finally fell into place for them or the other person or people finally changed their attitude toward them. They fall straight back into feeling they had nothing to do with it and they were not the cause, until I remind them of the many days of using the creative process preceding the fulfilled desire. Even then, they still have trouble really believing the whole thing about the Force. It was easy for me to accept the knowledge, because I had been witness to many great things that I had created in my life. At times, because the whole concept sounds somewhat bizarre or weird, I was sure some people thought I was a bit crazy. Many believed it was physical or the events that led up to the outcome were the cause. I explained over and over again it was the controlled daydreaming carried out in our imagination with all the senses and attention to detail that brought about the desired outcome. The events were just the dots we joined together. We are the cause every time without fail.

There are major factors to ensure that you are emitting crystal-clear high frequencies via the Force from your thoughts and feelings, and they are gratitude, forgiveness, and judgment. As you continue to read on, you will understand their importance to the creative process.

> All that we are is the result of what we have thought. The mind is everything. What we think, we become.

> —Maharishi Mahesh Yogi

> The world of reality has its limits; the world of imagination is boundless.

> —Jean-Jacques Rousseau

Readers notes

Chapter Five

Gratitude

Gratitude is so very important to clear the frequency waves, raise vibration, and open the channels for oneself. Some of us live our lives without gratitude for anything we receive in life. It's only when something is taken away from us—and this could be anything—that we realize how good it was to have that someone or that something in our lives. It's also like the minute you feel you might lose that special someone in your life, your job, or something like your business, the value of that someone or something appreciates tenfold, and you feel extremely appreciative to have that person or that thing dear to you.

Many may turn to pray at this point and begin to thank God, source energy, the higher self, infinite intelligence, or whatever they may refer or name their belief in life. Some are grateful for what they already have in life and give thanks for it daily. I know I do, and it makes me feel amazing. You see, gratitude is a very important part of your vibration of energy, and when you are grateful on a daily basis, you increase your vibration and therefore emit a high-frequency wave, tuning you in to a frequency via the Force to receive great things and have much more to be thankful for in life.

When you constantly give thanks for all that you are and have, you maintain a positive vibration in the energy sphere of your body. This energy is creative energy, and you will experience seeing many things appearing in your life from your thoughts and feelings about your desires. The more you practice the feeling of gratitude, the more your desires will appear in your reality.

The best way to express gratitude in life is to take some time out to ponder all the things you have been blessed with and are grateful for. When anything is not quite going my way or I feel a bit of a victim, I do this. Most of the time, I write a list of things about my life I am grateful for. You've heard the saying "Count your blessings." You see, when you focus on your list, you are giving it attention in your mind and therefore creating through your imagination more things to be grateful for. You have read the phrase "Where focus goes, energy flows." It means that whatever you give your attention to will appear in kind in your reality.

Here is a practical and very productive exercise for you. Write down on a daily basis a list of what you are grateful for in your life. I find it really sets you up for a great day and puts things in your life in order of importance.

For example, my list would look something like this:

I am extremely thankful for my children's health.
I am extremely thankful for my health.
I am extremely thankful for my family and friends.
I am extremely thankful for nature.
I am extremely thankful for the air I breathe.
I am extremely thankful for my home.
I am extremely thankful for the water I drink and wash with.
I am extremely thankful for the food I eat.
I am extremely thankful for my bed.
I am extremely thankful for my car.

I am extremely thankful for my business and money.
And so on...

When you finish your gratitude list, you will feel a shift in the way you feel, a feeling of bliss, contentment, and peacefulness. This is your vibration increasing and emitting a higher frequency via the Force. Your mind feels more orderly, and you begin to think positive thoughts as your perception of things in your life takes on an order of importance. Negative clutter in the mind starts to fade and the feelings of stress along with it, leaving you feeling relaxed all over and truly grateful and healthy.

Being grateful is the most powerful frequency you can emit in order to sustain the Force working to your advantage; all your desires will appear in your life in abundance and in a shorter period of time.

> Be thankful for what you have; you'll end up having more.
> If you concentrate on what you don't have, you will never,
> ever have enough.
>
> —Oprah Winfrey

> The roots of all goodness lie in the soil of appreciation for
> goodness.
>
> —Dalai Lama

> The grateful mind is constantly fixated upon the best.
> Therefore, it tends to become the best. It takes the form
> or character from the best, and will receive the best.
>
> —Wallace D. Wattles

Gratitude is an attitude that hooks us up to our source of supply. And the more grateful you are, the closer you become to your maker, to the architect of the universe, to the spiritual core of your being. It's a phenomenal lesson.

—Bob Proctor

Readers notes

Chapter Six

My Student Creates Her Perfect Job

I was at a supermarket that I regularly visit, when I got to talking to a checkout woman who remarked on how happy and positive I was being with her in conversation. Well, I told her it's very important to me to feel good as often as I can for reasons that could take a while to explain. As she was dealing with my items, I noticed she seemed reasonably positive, so I asked her how she was feeling.

She replied, "I am fine, thanks, but will be glad when it's five o'clock and time to go home."

I told her she should really enjoy her job, and she replied, "Well, I don't really. Would you after ten years of doing the same thing?"

I replied, "OK, I understand, but is this job what you really want to do in life, or is it a means to an end?"

She replied, "No, it's not, but it's a job. It pays the bills just about."

I said to her, "You know you should love what you do in life, so what is it you would really love to do?"

She replied, "I am a trained teaching assistant, and I would really like to work with children with learning difficulties, but it's hard to find positions like that."

I thought to myself, "I must share with her the knowledge of the Force. It will not only help her but help others she is qualified to help."

I said to her, "Is it truly your heart's desire to do that job as an occupation?"

She said, "Yes. Why? Do you know any jobs like that available?"

I said, "No, but I can help you to get whatever you want in life."

I told her she could have anything she desired.

She replied, "I have tried to get jobs like those but failed all the time. How can you help?"

I told her she was doing it all the wrong way and there was a creative process to have, be, or do anything in life. I was happy to share with her my knowledge. Well, she stopped working for a few minutes on her checkout, and I had her full attention.

She responded, "OK. How on earth can I do that?"

I told her she had to change her mind-set, change how she thought and felt about her circumstances.

I said, "Firstly, you're doing something you don't like, that makes you feel bad and dissatisfied, and really you should be feeling happy and grateful that you are gainfully employed, because for the moment, it's working well for you. This will give you a good feeling, which is important for this creative process."

I told her once she had established this positive feeling and opened up her mind, she needed to find some time to be alone where she wouldn't be disturbed at home, preferably sitting down in a comfortable chair or lying in bed before sleeping at night, which is even better. (OK, a note to you, the reader, at this point; this is a good time for you to take notes and accept this as a practical lesson of instruction that you may choose to use to create your perfect job opportunity.)

Right, carrying on, I then explained to her once she had quietened her mind, she needed to focus on her desire in her mind's eye, so in this case it was the job she always wanted to have. I instructed her to see herself already having the job, in the event as herself, actually playing out the job description in her imagination, not as an observer but being herself as it would be if it were real life. "Feel the atmosphere," I told her. "Hear the sounds of the children's laughter, the screaming and shouting in the class-room. Speak with them, see them looking at you as you lecture them, and smell the smells you would smell in a typical classroom. You will drift into what I call a controlled daydream. You will at some point feel as though you are truly in that atmosphere, a state of mind that feels totally real to you. Think of your old job while you are there as an old memory, feeling grateful that you have a new job now, and you are enjoying it immensely. Feel the feelings of appreciation from the children, and feel the excitement of knowing you are finally doing something you truly wanted to do all your life. You can't believe it's happened." I reminded her she is herself in her controlled dream, not an observer. It's very important to note that. Make sure you involve as much detail as possible so as to experience the whole episode as if it were real. You may feel a feeling of detachment and bliss, almost like you are elsewhere, not where you are physically but still present. Feel your desire unfolding in front of you and all around you. When all the sensations are present, you are truly creating via the Force. You become one with the Force, and when you exit your controlled dream, your body may feel somewhat stiff; this is normal when emerging from deep thought.

> When you visualize, then you materialize. If you've been there in the mind, you'll go there in the body.
>
> —Denis Waitley

I told her to do this twice daily for as long as it took until eventually she experienced the whole episode appearing in her reality. Well, a week later, I was back at the store checking out on a different checkout, and she got my attention and called me over.

She said, "I just wanted to say thank you, as I have felt so different after our talk, so uplifted and positive."

I replied, "I am glad to hear it. Have you started the creative process yet?"

She replied, "Not yet, but I will be on it this week for sure."

I said to her, "Don't throw away this valuable information. You will be glad of the outcome."

Anyway, it transpires that she went off and did exactly what I told her to do, and about three weeks later, she called me over to cash out on her checkout, as she had something important to tell me.

She said with so much joy on her face, "You are not going to believe what I am about to tell you!"

I replied, "I am all ears. Give it to me. What's happened since we last spoke?"

"Well," she said, "I can't believe I have only have one week left to work here, as I have been accepted for a job at a school down the road for children with special needs. It's perfect for me!"

Well, she received exactly what she wanted in life.

I replied, "That's amazing! I am pleased for you."

She said, "I followed your instructions and went into a controlled day-dream, and I was in it for sure. It was real, I tell you; then just last week, I received a call from an old friend out of the blue who told me she had put my name forward for a job opportunity that she knew about, because it was a good match for me. Anyway, they called me up, and yeah, after a brief interview, I was accepted there and then."

I explained to her that was how it all came together. The Force will create the doors to open, the events, the telephone calls, the circum-stances, and the people who appear in your life to show you the way to receive your fulfilled desire. This is the Force in action.

She said, "I can believe it. It definitely worked for me."

I replied, "I have done this for most of my life, and you can do it for anything, just *anything*. Big or small, it really does not matter."

She was extremely delighted, and I felt very happy for her.

> Nurture your mind with great thoughts, for you will never
> go any higher than you think.

> —Benjamin Disraeli

Readers notes

Chapter Seven

Forgiveness

Forgiveness is another key factor for creating optimum health and happiness.

I would explain to my students that forgiveness is one of the most important elements of the use of the Force. When you forgive someone, you are letting go of negative energy you have been carrying around with you in your body's energy sphere. You are releasing the negative emotion that is blocking the flow of energy in your energy field, preventing anything you desire via Force from appearing in your life.

Forgiveness can be done through meditation any time of the day, morning or night, or perhaps in person by simply saying, "I forgive you," if you are still in a position to do that. Even if it's not your fault, as long as you feel forgiveness in your heart and mind, no matter how bad the memory, you can let it go and feel the shift in your energy field and the pressure lift off your shoulders from the change in energy.

Holding on to any negative memories will only create more of the same via the Force and will hold you back from receiving whatever you desire in life. It can also make you unwell, as we know the body is an expression of the mind, and that's why some people look very miserable, depressed, aged, and tired; they are carrying around with them negative feelings and thoughts. So forgive, make peace with yourself, and then focus all your attention on gratitude and positive things in your life right now. Then, you can expect a change of good things to come.

Forgiveness is what propels the manifestation process of all your desires via the Force. You will feel liberated once you forgive, as it releases the negative energy immediately, and you will feel a great shift to a better place with a different mind-set. You will feel compassion for others in your life and a sense of humbleness without the ego.

I have met people who have hung on to negative thoughts and emotions from past events throughout their lives, and they don't realize how unhealthy it's making them feel. They don't take advice to forgive very well, and they continue to hold on to the negative baggage, resentment, and anger that grind them down with ill health. This attitude eventually produces diseases in the body, which have catastrophic effects that can lead them to an early grave.

Let go of the hateful thoughts, the bitterness, the grudges, and the resentment. Let it all go. It does you absolutely no favors in life. It's pure self-destruction to harbor these bad thoughts in your mind. It creates a negative vibration in your energy sphere that blocks all the good things from showing up in your reality via the Force.

People don't realize how these negative feelings hold them back from living the life they were born to live. Once you get past your ego and forgive, you will feel so free. You will always want to forgive and let go. As you move through life, you will become aware of your thoughts and won't entertain any negative thinking, for a better, healthier, and a more abundant life. It is only then you will live a life of full potential and fulfillment.

I find it really doesn't take much to have a pleasing personality in life when you are filled with loving and caring thoughts for all. Forgive and let go of whatever you are holding on to and choose to send love instead, so you can open yourself up to receiving love, a healthier vibration of energy via the Force.

> When you forgive, you in no way change the past—but you sure do change the future.
>
> —Bernard Meltzer

> I can be changed by what happened to me, but I refuse to be reduced by it.
>
> —Maya Angelou

Readers notes

Chapter Eight

Jealousy

For me, jealousy has to be one of the most negative vibrations of energy a person can emit via the Force.

I must say, I have never been envious of anyone in this world. In fact, I always get more inspired and empowered by what someone has achieved in life, whatever it may be. Jealousy is a belief that has been programmed into a person's mind at a young age, and it becomes that person's thoughts, feelings, and actions later on in life. Some people are jealous of others for having a nice home, an expensive car, a nice partner, a great body, good looks, talents, a thriving business, and so on. They sometimes make it blatantly obvious they are envious of that person by ignoring him or her or talking negatively about him or her with others. A typical example of jealousy we have all experienced at some point in life is maybe a friend, neighbor, or work colleague who didn't comment on perhaps our nice home, new car, that great vacation we just returned from with a great tan, newly purchased clothing, or a new hairstyle. The person deliberately ignores the fact and says nothing. He or she pretends not to notice. You see, it's really because jealous people feel they deserve it too. It's not about you; it's what you are or have. He or she maintains a "Why you? Why not me?" attitude, and it makes him or her form negative thought patterns in the mind, which become a habitual way of thinking toward all well-to-do, successful, and fortunate people.

You have to prepare yourself for this situation when you become successful and fulfill your desires in life; you will lose people along the way. They disappear from your life and drop out of your reality slowly but surely, mainly because you have moved on and bettered your life, for example, with a new job, success, more money, a bigger house, a nicer car or cars, a different circle of prosperous friends, more travel, and so on. They realize they can't keep up with you, and in their eyes, you have changed. "You're not the same," they say or think, and they have remained the same in the comfortable old place where you once were. So you will find they don't bother with you anymore. I know this from experience, I can tell you. I gained a whole new circle of friends when I became prosperous. My old circle of friends just fell to the wayside. They failed to keep in touch, even when I did my best to share my wealth and treat them the same. It just didn't seem to work. I'd created a new life for myself, and I had to start living it without them.

Jealousy is a form of resentment toward another, begrudging a person for having something one would like oneself. One of the main things people are jealous of is that people who are rich seem to have everything in life. They harbor beliefs that rich people are all crooks, evil, dishonest, just very lucky, or born with a silver spoon in their mouths. These are beliefs that were passively programmed by their environment when they were younger from maybe parents, relatives, friends, the media, and so on, and it has become their way habitual way of thinking. They have formed limiting beliefs later in life, which are very disempowering and destructive.

I must stress to you this: if you feel you possess these limiting beliefs, get rid of them fast, because they're holding you back and creating a negative vibration in your energy sphere, prohibiting great things from manifesting in your life via the Force. Jealousy is a negative low frequency that cancels out any positive high frequencies that bring to you good fortune.

This negative vibration is emitting a low frequency that will only bring you more experiences via the Force to be jealous of. Whenever I see people with what I would like to have or be in life, whatever it may be—a nice car, a beautiful home, a great business, or even nice clothing—I praise them and say to myself or to them in person, "Good luck to you," even if I don't know how they obtained their material wealth. I just wish them well, as it's a better frequency to emit and will only return good experiences to me in many ways via the Force. Plus it will make me feel empowered and good to know I felt positive toward another person and not envious. Prosperous people like to be complimented and admired; they're only human after all.

I have known some people who are literally sick with envy. They just can't help thinking and feeling that way, and its pure sabotage on their behalf. Most jealous people just don't know it, as it's buried deep in their subconscious mind. I believe jealousy is a disease, and it's a very destructive vibration of energy to retain in your field. It can make you very ill in the long run. Be inspired to have it all yourself one day, not jealous or hopeful to see someone lose it all. It's better for you all around.

Readers notes

Chapter Nine

Judgment

A very important factor to be aware of in maintaining a high vibration of energy is not being judgmental toward other people, situations, ideas, appearances, and possessions.

Judging in a negative way is common in life, but it's very detrimental to our energy field as it alters the state of our thoughts, feelings, and attitudes. We judge someone we meet (or even from afar) within milliseconds. We build an image in our minds of what we think of the person and label him or her instantaneously, purely from appearances. This happens several times a day without us knowing who the person really is, what he or she is like as a person, or how he or she really acts.

We judge our family, coworkers, bosses, friends, total strangers, what we see on TV or the Internet, and what we hear on the radio. When we are focused on negative beliefs about someone, something, or a situation and we rehearse these thoughts constantly, we will find that the person, thing, or situation will transpire in that manner.

You may find yourself at times saying, "I was right about that person. I'm a good judge of character." Well, whatever you hold in your imagination about someone or something, either way, you are correct. You may be thinking, "We don't always get it right. Sometimes we're a bad judge of character." Well, you will find unconsciously or consciously, the frequency emitted from the energy of your thoughts and feelings via the Force will always be perfectly tuned to whatever the outcome of your judgment is. You will at times unconsciously doubt your own judgment from your true beliefs, which stems from your mental programming.

I refer to my student, mentioned in the Introduction, who had issues in his mind about his boss being negative and ignorant toward him. Well, the more he judged him to be that way in his mind, the more it would be so in his reality, therefore fulfilling his belief, making it true. It was only when he changed his negative judgment to a positive one and imagined his boss being pleasant and positive with him that his boss behaved that way toward him in reality.

As you change your thoughts and feelings, the frequency emitted will create via the Force and reflect back your judgment in kind, confirming you as being correct in your thinking.

You see, being judgmental in a positive way increases your vibration in your energy sphere around your body and emits a high frequency via the Force, therefore creating positivity in your reality. Negative judgments cause a low vibration in your energy sphere around your body, which then emits a low frequency via the Force, fulfilling negativity in your reality.

If you want to maintain a positive high vibration, it's best to monitor your thoughts as best you can and praise people. See the good in all. Don't run down, criticize, find fault, or discredit people for who they are, what they are, or what they want to be in life, as it does not serve you well to do so.

Remember, we are all energy. That means we are all one, one infinite ocean of energy connected to one supply: the Force. The invisible Force creates all we know to be in existence and continues to keep alive all that exists. It is constantly expanding life throughout the universe and beyond our comprehension.

Have you ever noticed how so many things start to break down around us when we are constantly moaning and complaining all the time?

We sometimes judge our possessions in a negative way, and as we do, because everything is energy, it somehow breaks down on us and we then find ourselves saying, "I knew it. I knew it was going to break. It's old. It's useless. It's had it." We don't realize that our thoughts and feelings with focused intention create the frequency emitted from our energy field via the Force, which makes the very thing to break.

Some old folks call it the evil eye or say it must have been jinx. It's the power of our minds imprinting our very thoughts and feelings via the Force. I want to take you back to the first chapter and remind you that you may be thinking it's a coincidence it broke down or that it was going to break down anyway, but it isn't. It's the Force in action. It is always in motion, creating everything that happens.

I was looking at my car one day, and I do appreciate everything I have in my life and give gratitude for all I have, but it happened to me. I had a thought one day about my car that it was time maybe to upgrade it, as something potentially might go wrong with it, accompanied by an impulsive feeling of fear that something would go wrong with it. Lo and behold, two weeks later, the onboard computer broke down and needed a very costly fix. I knew when it happened my thoughts and feelings had created it, so it's important to be aware of your judgment toward every-thing in life—and I mean *everything*. Praise everyone and everything. Be grateful for all you have in life, and then you can be sure to create an abundance of positive experiences, relationships, and material wealth via the Force.

Our imagination is always creating our experiences every second of our waking life.

What you bless you multiply, what you condemn you lose.

—Stuart Wilde

When you judge another, you do not define them, you define yourself.

—Wayne Dyer

Whatever the mind of man can conceive and believe, it can achieve.

—Napoleon Hill

Readers notes

Chapter Ten

Assumption

We constantly make assumptions about others, situations, or ourselves. It's part of our habitual way of thinking. It's whether your assumption is positive or negative that decides the circumstances you experience in life.

When we make an assumption, we enter into a mini trance where our mind thinks in pictures and sounds, and we visualize and hear a story in our minds, playing out the way we think it's going to play out like a short movie. For example, if your general mood is one of a negative feeling, you will assume the worst outcome, whereas if your general mood is a positive one, you will assume a positive outcome in the story you are playing out in your mind in a brief trance. It's a controlled daydream but much shorter and more intense, as it carries all the senses of reality, giving it more amplification. This, by the way, is a very powerful creative process, as it ignites all the senses we have, causing a very strong vibration of energy in our energy sphere around our body. It emits a very clear, definitive frequency via the Force, creating the equivalent story in reality so it appears in one's daily life, and sometimes it creates instantaneously.

People assume the role of who they are from their thought patterns and resonate with one another through waves of vibrating energy. It's not uncommon to see two negative people gravitate to one another and spend time together, as their frequencies are in harmony. They think and talk about the same negative thoughts, whereas it's the opposite for positive people. Their frequencies harmonize with those of people who are positive thinkers and talkers. On a physical plane, we see this as people with commonalities. Your mood and state of mind are a vibration of energy; your reality is a true reflection of your mood and state of mind.

I had a student who assumed in his thoughts and in speech that a party he was invited to one evening was going to be a disaster for many reasons—the venue was small, certain friends wouldn't show up, food was going to be bad, and not enough drinks would be available. Well, this was his assumption, and he had clearly played out this whole scene in his mind with negative intentions and feelings. As he did this, his assumption became a firm belief in his mind to the point he was convinced it was a given fact, and no one could sway his assumption otherwise.

Well, the obvious appeared in his reality. It was a small venue, friends he wanted to be there did not show up, the food was bad, and the drinks were scarce. He had successfully created his assumption into fact and, with great pride, proclaimed to me, "I knew it would turn out that way!" believing his predictions were correct. Little did he know he had created his own fate from his assumption via the Force. I believe that predictions are nothing but creative processes carried out through the human imagination, and if you predict and assume anything with belief, it will materialize, therefore becoming a self-fulfilling prophecy. Here is a good exercise to carry out first thing every morning while getting ready for the day ahead. Assume out loud that your day has gone really well with positive encounters, as if your day has already happened and it's been a great day. Assume with belief that it has, and watch your day unfold. If you are in an occupation in sales, this practice should serve you well.

Assumptions and judgment really go hand in hand. a person is going to behave in such a manner, then thoughts and feelings, that person will present himself or herself in that way in our reality. It's important to be aware of your assumptions and correct them immediately for a positive and pleasing outcome. It works well because, as I have already outlined, this brief controlled trance, coupled with intense emotional feelings, emits a powerful and concise frequency, delivering a quick and accurate response in kind via the Force.

If you assume with certainty the job is going to be bad for whatever reason, or the interview will turn out unsuccessful, it shall be that way.

If you assume the holiday will not be pleasurable but boring, it will be. Your thoughts and feelings control the outcome of your assumption every time.

It works for self too. If you believe you are wealthy, confident, and successful and you assume the role, it will reflect as so in your reality. It works equally well for the opposite. Assume you lack confidence, you're broke and unsuccessful, and you shall experience it. You may have heard of the "act as if" principle. Well, act as if you are already that person even if you're not until you assume the role in life. Many people use this technique in business, and it works well. You will know if it's working, as people will respond to you differently, because their perception of you will have changed.

The Force will only create a true reflection of your assumption, state of mind, mood, and imagination, which create the fact. So never assume the worst of someone, yourself, or any situation. Have an optimistic and positive outlook on life and assume the best of everything and everyone.

Your assumption, to be effective, cannot be a single isolated act; it must be a maintained attitude of the wish fulfilled.

—Neville Goddard

Every moment of your life, consciously or unconsciously, you are assuming a feeling.

—Neville Goddard

Readers notes

Chapter Eleven

Perception

Perception is very powerful. It's the ability to become aware of something through our senses. When we perceive someone or something in a certain way, it becomes our thought pattern, and as we think and feel from our perception, we are emitting a frequency from our energy field via the Force, thus creating the very thing we perceive into an objective fact in our life experience. It becomes your personal reality to you and no one else.

Two people looking at the same situation will perceive the situation very differently and then construct their own thoughts of what they see or experience. I have experienced this; by changing my perception on any situation, person, or thing, it changes completely and miraculously. One of my students would constantly describe to me his job as being boring and unfulfilling, and the people he worked with appeared the same way to him. I explained to him that his perception was creating his experience. When his perception became his belief, it then caused a vibration in his energy field to emit a frequency via the Force, thus creating a true reflection in his reality. I told him to alter his perception of what he saw and heard with optimism, and he could expect to experience a whole new world with the same job and the same people he worked with. Well, he went about doing just what I explained to him, and he was amazed at the transformation. He could not believe how this minor change inside his mind could cause such a big change on the outside.

You see, it goes back to assuming and prejudging in our reality and building a story in our imagination from our perception of what we see, hear, and feel. As we conclude a belief in our mind as fact, we then create it in kind via the Force to appear in our reality. When you change the way you view things, they appear different on the screen of life. So if you have a positive perception of life, you can expect positive results every time. Once an employee of mine viewed his sales job as being hard and laborious, and another employee of mine looked at the same job as being challenging and rewarding. Well, the latter employee achieved great results and reaped a lot of commission and bonuses, but my other employee failed at the job and made very little. It was only when he changed his perception about the job and perceived himself as doing well that he started to achieve good results and make money. His perception became a hardened fact in his reality via the Force in action.

Some people's perception of life can be a cycle of negativity brought about from their negative thinking; their negative perception becomes their thought pattern. This pattern then becomes their projection of energy from what they have seen and heard, thus becoming their perception once more of what appears in their lives. Their thoughts and feelings are in a cycle, which creates the same experiences all over again. As mentioned earlier, unless you change your perception on whatever it may be, you will keep experiencing the same conditions in your life. This, by the way, is what keeps many people stuck in their ways for most of their lives, missing out on the very things they dream about and desire in life. This cycle of negativity makes people resentful by nature, which again leads to an unhealthy existence if left unchecked.

If you are confronted by a negative situation, never react to it in kind, as it will trigger negative emotions and feelings that will create more negative experiences to appear in your life. Respond in a way that will neutralize or diffuse the negative energy by rehearsal in the mind. (Read the chapter "How to Rehearse the Past").

> If you change the way you look at things, the things you look at change.
>
> —Wayne Dyer

Readers notes

Chapter Twelve

How to Heal Oneself via the Force

We hear of people who just miraculously get better for no apparent reason from a life-changing health condition after doctors said there was no hope and they just had to live with it. They would prescribe the usual medicines, such as painkillers, antidepressant tablets, creams, or whatever they believed was required to suppress the symptoms or sedate the pain. What about the root cause?

Well, I have come to learn from experience and exploration that we are the cure; we are always the cure, if we believe it to be so. We have had the knowledge and the ability to heal ourselves for centuries. If you explore Middle Eastern healing, Far Eastern medicine, and the Native American methods, you will see that they understood how to heal themselves, and they knew natural ways to use the Force to get well and achieve perfect health in the body. They still use their healing methods to this day.

I am not saying what I believe is the final word or the answer to all cases. I have the utmost respect for the medical profession, as medical intervention may be the only solution when symptoms have reached levels of concern and may be life threatening, such as heart failure, blood clots, or tumors. I just know I have used the creative Force to get other people's health back on track, and I constantly use it for my own health. It works very well and gives great results. You may have heard of mind over matter and the placebo effect in which medicine is replaced with sugar pills and the results are the same if not better. Some people get better after seeing the doctor, and all he or she has done is reassure them that they will be fine in a few days. Well, it's the belief factor that starts the healing process in motion. When you see yourself getting better or healed in the mind, that vision is expressed in the body and you start to feel better and regain your health. I believe prevention is better than cure, so it's good to keep focused on good-feeling thoughts and maintain a health-conscious mind. The saying goes, "Healthy body, healthy mind." I prefer to say, "Healthy mind, healthy body."

Let me give you some examples, and then I will run through the creative process for you to try out for yourself, as and when you may wish to do so.

You see, the body and mind are one. When you have aches, pains, or rashes in the body, they are an expression of the mind. They are fed from some emotional block stored in the mind. If you have a lot of disorder going on in the mind, it will show up in the body in the same way as some kind of health disorder, such as disease or pain, because the mind expresses itself in the body. If you are constantly stressed out from negative thinking created by your environment, you will feel it in the body in the form of tension, strains, headaches, and other possible symptoms.

Any negative thoughts rehearsed over and over in the mind will create negative energy in the body, which translates into physical illness of the body, and whatever symptoms you are experiencing are an expression of this disease. When these symptoms become prominent and consistent, they create total discomfort in the body. The sensations from these symptoms are unpleasant and cause us to feel negative emotions. We feel bad and produce more negative thoughts, which feed the condition even more. It's like the body becomes the mind and feeds the unhealthy condition itself. This, by the way, becomes a vicious cycle that can keep you trapped in bad health for many years.

I had a client who had a case of *Helicobacter pylori*, a bacterial growth in the stomach from food or water contamination. Anyone who has it will know it can lead to all kinds of unpleasant and painful feelings in the body. It can affect the digestive track in more ways than one, causing stomach ulcers, acid reflux, gastritis, depression, mind fog, and many other issues.

The disease is caused by an overgrowth of bacteria that lies in the stomach lining, causing damage to the bottom part of the stomach. It can form mini ulcers. He took prescribed medicine the first time he was diagnosed with it, and it seemed to clear it up for a short while, but it raised its ugly head again months later. Anyway, he didn't wish to take any more medicine to treat it because of the side effects, and I realized that at the time it showed up again, he had a lot of negative thoughts processing in his mind, and as he focused on one particular thought that truly bothered him, it would trigger the feeling of pain even more in his stomach area from the overproduction of acid.

I believed there and then this was the root cause of the symptoms expressed in his stomach region. As a neurolinguistic practitioner (NLP) and an emotional freedom technique (EFT), I understand that negative energy in the mind, conscious or subconscious, will express itself in the body, and the stomach is usually the first area to be affected, especially from the thought energy of worry, doubt, fear, anger, resentment, bitterness, and any other emotional traumas. You see, when our mind isn't right, as in a state of disorder and chaos, from maybe the loss of a loved one or a breakup in a relationship of some kind, money worries, job insecurity, or any other deep-rooted problem in our lives, we feel the sensations in the pit of our stomach as pain, and we tend to feel sick and lose our appetite, which leads to other health conditions.

Whenever I feel somewhat unhealthy, I set about using the creative process to heal myself and clear up the symptoms that are causing me discomfort and bad feelings and the negative thoughts that are feeding my health condition. I carry out this process usually before I sleep at night, lying down or sitting comfortably in my armchair. With absolutely no disturbances, I begin to put myself in a state of relaxation and calm.

I first perform a brief session on gratitude and forgiveness (please refer to the chapters on these topics, as they are of prime importance to the healing process). Next, I clear my mind of any negative thoughts by silencing my mind of any chatter by focusing my mind on my breathing and heartbeat. Once in a state of well-being and calm, I begin to create, in my mind's eye, a controlled daydream of myself in great health. I feel what it feels like to be in optimal health. I am myself in my imagination, not an observer, seeing and hearing family, friends, and colleagues saying things like "You look really good." I would reply, "Thanks! I feel better than ever." I experience in my controlled daydream all the feelings and sensations of great physical health, imagining my reality, whatever it may be, with gratitude and kindness, giving no expression to anything remotely negative during this creative session. I also hear myself saying things like "I remember when I wasn't feeling very well" and reflect on it as a very distant memory. After a while, I come back to a semiawakened state of mind and proceed to sleep in this relaxed and comfortable state, knowing I am in great health. If, for any reason, with any of these creative sessions, you become mentally distracted by conflicting thoughts, as will happen from time to time, because your reality will remind you of the conditions the way they really are, refocus and start again until you complete your session and feel it to be as real as it would be if it were played out in reality.

I carry out these sessions for as long as it takes until it becomes a fact. I am conscious of my eating habits too, concentrating on a nutritious diet, as what you feed the mind is equally important as what you feed the body. When I start to feel better, the more I believe it, the healthier

I become. The last time I carried out this process after creating good health, I went to the doctor to get a blood test to see if my problem was resolved. I was clear. I have continued to use this process for great health in the mind and the body to this day. I'm always amazed by the results created via the Force. I find myself sharing this story and creative process with anyone I speak to, who has some kind of health issue. The feedback so far has been incredible, as the people who have followed the process have experienced phenomenal results, including my student with the stomach problem, mentioned earlier in this chapter.

Looking into a mirror first thing in the morning, and telling yourself you look great and are in fine physical health three to four times does wonders to your state of mind and being. Many prominent people have used the mirror technique throughout history. It has been mentioned by many authors in their books. I do believe it is all a matter of belief.

As you believe, so it shall be done unto you.

—Jesus Christ

Sometimes it's just a belief, a knowing that the Force will take care of us throughout our waking life. It always fascinates me how all our cuts and grazes just miraculously heal up and go away, like they never happened, and we do nothing but observe this miracle. To me, this is a testament that there is an invisible Force, a power for the benefit of all creation, large or small.

One case that stands out was a parent I would see from time to time at my children's school. He walked with a metal walking stick and complained of being in a lot of pain in his hip. He talked about how it made his life quite miserable. He had tried various treatments to overcome the pain and regain normal use of his leg, but nothing seemed to work, and he continued to take painkillers for the pain.

Well, one day, I asked him, "How's the leg?"

He began to give me the whole story of his leg and how nothing worked well in the medical treatment he received. I felt the need to share my experience and explain the creative process to him, and how the body would heal itself if he believed it to be true.

I gave him instructions that he was to focus his attention in his mind's eye in a controlled daydream, and in his situation, he would be himself, acting or playing out a scene in which he was walking properly without the aid of a walking stick. He was to feel the freedom and the pain-free feelings in his leg, along with all the other senses as if it were being played out in his reality.

I told him to see, feel, and act as he would if his leg were cured and see the expressions on his family's faces as he walked toward them. I advised him to hear their positive comments and feel the emotion of joy as he ran with his grandchildren in the local park. I told him to add as much detail as possible and feel gratitude for having great health. Also he was to have a brief reflection on a past memory when his leg was in pain, how it was difficult to walk, and believe that it was all in the past now. Believe you are cured and in fine physical health, and it's a done deal. I told him to do this session just before he slept at night after a brief meditation on gratitude and forgiveness and for at least a month or as long as required until it became an objective fact in his world.

Well, he was eager to carry out this instruction, and it was weeks before I saw him again, but when I did, he couldn't wait to tell me how great he felt, as he no longer required a walking stick, though he still had a slight hobble. He said he carried out the process for quite a while, and then he noticed less and less pain and could put more pressure on his leg. It was as if it had happened by itself; he never really made any reference to my instructions much, other than he said he had done it several times. I knew it was the process of the Force in action that cured him, as he believed in it so much it became a fact in his reality.

As it is said, we create our own reality. I noticed that we have the ability to create for others in our own imagination. All you have to do during the controlled daydream is visualize people getting better and hear them say they feel much better. Expect to see them in optimal health, and you will. Many don't realize this, but they have effectively done this through prayer maybe for a member of the family or friend at some point in their life with the same outcome. The imagination coupled with unwavering faith and belief creates miracles via the Force.

> I have decided to be happy, because it's good for my health.
>
> —Voltaire

Readers notes

Chapter Thirteen

Many Might Call This a Miracle

I was overwhelmed by the news from this particular person using the creative process and allowing the Force to create her thoughts and feelings into a miracle.

One of my students, whom I have mentioned earlier in this book, landed her dream job using my instructions to create via the Force. She came to me one day and asked me if this process works for anything. I told to her that it works for anything you put your mind on. She explained to me her desire to have a child; she and her partner had been trying for many years in spite of what several doctors had told her—that she had zero chance of conception.

Well, I went through the whole creative process once more and instructed her to get herself in a quiet place, imagine she was already pregnant, and get extremely excited about the whole event. You have to control the daydream in such a way that you play out the whole event like a movie in your mind's eye, the whole episode from start to finish. Being herself in this movie, she was to see what she would see, hear what she would hear, and feel what it felt like to see herself pregnant and ready to give birth. I told her to hear friends and family commenting on how pregnant she looked and feel the sensations of being pregnant. After a few weeks, I told her to do a session where she would go through the process of giving birth, feeling all the sensations of the aches and pains and see her baby all healthy, crying away, and the joy on the faces of all the nurses and her partner in the delivery room. I finally told her to practice this daily with plenty of detail until it became so.

Well, she was very motivated by what I had taught her to do, and she said, "I will definitely try it out. I have nothing to lose."

Two weeks later, I remember saying to her when she told me her new job was going really well that she had best get her maternity leave booked as a joke, which made her smile.

Three months later, even though I always have faith that it works every time if it's done correctly, I found myself doing a double take on the e-mail she sent me on a social media site. It read,

Just to let you know, it's been a while since we spoke. I'm pregnant, and it worked! I am two months pregnant and over the moon and the doctor can't believe it, neither can my husband or family. We can't believe it, thank you, I did what you said, saw myself pregnant etc.

I was overwhelmed by the news, and it gave me even more reason not to ever doubt the Force in action. It works every time, truly every time. I have yet to see it fail. It was almost a year since I spoke to her, but I noticed when looking on my social media, she had proudly posted pictures of her new baby boy, which was even more proof this process works.

The following is a personal story of the Force in action.

I was on vacation with my children in Spain. We had traveled there by plane. We had been there around two weeks, and I realized that as I booked my flight tickets on the Internet, which, by the way, is the procedure for most airlines, especially with the short charter flights, I had to confirm our seats on the return journey. Well, I should have confirmed the seats two weeks before departure to ensure we had seats allocated together, so as not to be split from our children or even have the children sitting with strangers, which would have proven to be an issue, as my children were very young. Well, my children realized I had not confirmed our seats in the recommended time frame before departure, and they became quite anxious and nervous.

I decided there and then I would use the creative Force and ensure all would be just fine. I did a session that night and imagined in my mind's eye that we were all seated together and in the comfort of first-class treatment. So we went the very next day to a location where there was an Internet connection to go online and confirm our seats, and as I was confirming the seats, it did not give me a choice of seating, just a confirmation they were booked. I remember my children were looking on with concern, but I was sure it was not going to be a problem. I remarked it was not a problem; we would be just fine. I also remember saying, "We not only have seats together, but we are traveling first class," and then I clicked the confirmation button and proceeded to the reception to pick up my printed boarding passes for our journey home.

To my delight and the excitement of my children, we were not only all seated together but we were seated at the front of the aircraft in row four. Even though this charter flight had only coach class throughout the aircraft, I noticed printed on the boarding passes we had priority boarding, which gave us access to the aircraft before any other passengers. It was an upgrade I had not paid for. It was just a great feeling that I had the faith and the knowledge to use the formidable Force to our complete advantage, and my children were amazed that the creative process works extremely well when you know how to perform it correctly.

Remember, we live in a universe of cause and effect. Well, the creative process in the mind, which I call a controlled daydream, is the cause and the effect is the result, your fulfilled desire. You don't ever have to know how it's going to happen. Don't wonder when it's going to happen. Just know definitively what you want, carry out the creative process as instructed in this book, and know and feel you have already experienced and have obtained your desire. In other words, believe it's happened and the Force will do its magic. Always maintain loyalty to your fulfilled desire, and ignore your current true state of affairs until change presents itself from the Force.

Every desire imagined will hatch within its own time period.

There are only two ways to live your life. One is as though nothing is a miracle. The other is as though everything is a miracle.

—Albert Einstein

Everyone visualizes whether he knows it or not. Visualizing is the great secret of success.

—Genevieve Berhrend

Reality is merely an illusion, albeit a very persistent one.

—Albert Einstein

Readers notes

Chapter Fourteen

Creating Your Perfect Relationship

Everyone in life wants to love and be loved unconditionally. It's human nature. It is said there is a man for every woman and a woman for every man in this world during anyone's lifetime. So then why are there so many single people out there or people who have so many relationships and none works out? We always tend to blame others for the problems in our relationships or our marriage failures, but it's not the case.

Here's the truth of the matter. We are totally responsible for all our failed relationships in life, whether we choose to believe it or not. I too struggled to believe that last comment, but it's true. Your partner who showed up in your life had to be imagined and created via the Force for him or her to appear in your reality. No one in this world can be drawn into your life unless you and you alone create it to happen. People appear by invitation only. Ever thought about someone you haven't seen in while and then out of the blue, he or she shows up or calls you? Well, it's the Force in action. It is not a coincidence; you created it.

You see, we all have certain criteria we look for in a person we would like to attract into our lives, for example, height, build, color of eyes, color of hair, certain type of look, personality, character, and so on. It's been said we tend to attract people who resemble our parents; for example, daughters tend to be attracted to men who look and act somewhat like their fathers, and the sons do the same with their mothers. This, by the way, is now a scientific fact. This data is rehearsed in our mind every time we think and hope to find that special someone to spend the rest of our lives with. When we imagine it happening with an open heart, emotionalized thoughts, and belief, not long after, we see that person show up, and it always feels like a coincidence. It was meant to be, and fate brought us together.

I have to tell you again; we are responsible for who shows up in our lives and also who leaves our lives. For example, if you have trust issues consciously or unconsciously with a partner and think and feel he or she maybe unfaithful in the relationship, you will be creating, through your imagination the very thing via the Force. Once it's imagined with the powerful emotions of worry, fear, and doubt, there is no stopping the Force from bringing it to life. So be careful what you think about and fixate upon. Keep your mind focused on the good in your relationship.

Imagination is the secret of life.

Here is an explanation of what I shared with some of my students after they approached me with the quest to find love via the Force. It gave them excellent results.

Firstly, it's important to know what kind of person you want in your life. We all know what we don't want; that's for sure. The key is to focus your imagination on what you *do* want. You may not have an image of this person in mind, so use an image of someone most likely to fit the description and personality you are most attracted to.

Find yourself a quiet place to go to for a while. And sitting or lying down, just before you go into sleep, carry out the creative process. Close your eyes, and through a controlled daydream start to imagine yourself in your mind's eye as yourself and not as an observer. This may sound repetitive, like previous instructions laid out in this book, but I can tell you it is necessary. It is like when a chef bakes a cake, if he or she leaves out any of the most important ingredients, you can be sure the cake won't turn out right. Besides, repetition is good for programming one's mind.

Play the part of yourself in your mind's eye, create the events as they would happen in your reality; see the ideal person you wish to be with; see how he or she looks, and hear how he or she sounds. Imagine how he or she smells (maybe of your favorite cologne) and feels to touch and his or her behavior with you. Have him or her speak to you, saying things like, "I'm so happy to be with you," or "You are just the kind of person I've been looking for."

The key is to make it feel as real as you can.

Give your mental movie scene all the emotional senses of how it would feel to you in reality, and get excited as if it's already happened, like you are with that person and have family members or friends commenting, "You look great together," or "You are made for each other."

Continue this process of events in your mind's eye for as long as you desire. Do this as often as you wish until it becomes a matter of fact in your reality. Watch how the Force goes to work for you, and observe your thoughts and feelings in your day-to-day life, holding true to your belief that your new partner already exists and is part of your life and that this imagined partner is but merely moments away from appearing in your life. When it happens, you will be surprised and feel totally surreal. You will believe it's just coincidence, and it was going to happen anyway.

You will believe your physical actions have caused this event to unfold and find it hard to believe that such a creative process in your imagination could result in such an amazing thing happening in your life. Well, the fact of the matter is, it was your doing. *You* are the cause. You are always the cause.

By the way, if you are in a relationship or marriage that is going through tough times or has lost its spark, you can use this powerful creative process to recreate the joy of love and happiness you once had back into the relationship. Recall all the good memories you once experienced with your partner, rehearse them over and over in your mind's eye, follow the creative process outlined earlier in this chapter, and watch how things start to change for the better. It will feel like the chemistry between you just came back by itself. You will feel your partner has changed for the better and give no credit to the creative process and events leading up to the desired outcome. The turn of events will feel bizarre as your relationship moves from misery to happiness with the same two people, but it's true. I've seen it over and over.

Remember to do this with an open heart, full of love for that person and yourself. Remember not to focus on any negative thoughts or current problems. Eliminate them from the mind completely. Focus only on how you want your relationship to be, and it will be so, especially as you believe it to be true in your imagination and you remain focused on your changed situation. See it as if it has already happened—as if it's a done deal, so to speak—and then watch it appear in your life experience. Don't worry about the how and when. Remember to just let it be, and it will unfold and happen naturally. This creative process will surely rejuvenate your relationship; however, if you leave it to chance, you will only see more of same unhappiness, failure, and perhaps separation.

New Relationship Story: Case Study

I had a student who just left a very toxic relationship where he saw no future. He came to me saying that he didn't want to be single but didn't want to attract the same type of partner into his life once more. I listened to all his concerns and proceeded to explain that the previous relationship was his creation. He tried to defend himself by saying he did everything he could to make it work but it was his partner, which was the cause of the breakdown in the relationship.

Well I had heard enough and wanted to help him to understand it was his fault entirely whether or not he felt he was a good husband and did his very best to keep his wife happy. I shared with him the knowledge of the Force and told him his entire negative past thoughts and conversations of his partner were the cause of all the negative experiences that appeared in his relationship right up to the bitter end. At that point he started to appreciate what I was trying to tell him,

When he changed his mind-set of what he thought and felt about his partner, he altered the energy from his negative thoughts emitting a low frequency via the Force, which created the very toxic relationship he went through. You see when you decide and believe anyone is no longer the person they used to be, whether it's a partner, a friend or business colleague, you start to create in your mind an assumption about him or her that they have changed for worse. When you focus your attention and energy on this matter, your perception of him or her starts to create in your mind a new characterization of the person in a way that you start to dislike, causing the whole episode from your perception to materialize in that manner. Once they become what you imagined them to be, you will react and respond to them in such a way that their behavior will match your thoughts and feeling of them. Once on this path, you will find it hard to reconcile your difference; however, if you truly wish to change the situation you can use the creative process to do so. (Earlier in this chapter I have explained how to rekindle a failing relationship.) When an individual leaves your reality, it's the Force in action—your creative imagination tuning you out of the frequency that once brought you together. Remember people show up in your life through invitation only and leave the same way via the Force from the creative process carried out in your imagination.

Well, I continued by saying, "Now you know the real reason behind the breakdown; let me explain how to create a new relationship with that in mind."

He was very interested to know how to use the knowledge, so I explained to him, "Firstly you need to know want kind of a person do you really want in your life and what do you want from the relationship."

He said "I want someone who is attractive, independent, has her own home, and enjoys the outdoors."

I said, "Well, that's clear enough," and I began to explain how to perform the creative process outlined earlier in this chapter.

He began to tell me what he didn't want in the relationship and I stopped him in his path and explained to him to avoid thinking and speaking of what he didn't want; it would sabotage the creative process of creating his dream relationship and will only create a relationship similar to the one he had just had.

Any way about a month later, he was all fired up as he decided to try out online dating, which he wasn't a big fan of but had the urge to try out. He had to his amazement four invitations which he took up, but failed to make a good connection with any of them. He called me up and explained that he was carrying out the creative process, but it was hard to stay focused all the time.

I explained, "When you get distracted, start again, but keep it simple and focus on what you want with all the detail and senses as though it's already happened. Make it feel as real as you can."

After a couple of weeks, he told me with excitement in his voice that one of the dates online contacted him again, the very least person he expected to do so and the one he was most fond of. "It was like fate brought us together," he said. "She is just what I imagined to be: she loves the outdoor, has her own home, a great profession, attractive, and wants to get serious." He was so excited he just felt it was meant to be, and fate brought them together. "It was the Force that did the magic," I said. "It works well, doesn't it? Your very thoughts, feelings, and actions have transpired in your reality. Your partner and relationship is a carbon copy of your mind, a true reflection of your imagination." Others too I know have experienced such results when using the creative process correctly.

> See the things that you want as already yours. Know that they will come to you at need. Then let them come. Don't fret and worry about them. Don't think about your lack of them. Think of them as yours, as belonging to you, as already in your possession.

> —Robert Collier

Readers notes

Chapter Fifteen

Conversations in the Mind

When we use mind and speech together in harmony with our emotions, miracles can happen. All human beings have mind conversations throughout their waking life. It's the most natural thing to do, next to breathing and sleeping, but some people have the ability to control their conversations, and some who meditate can quiet the chatter in their minds completely, which has many positive effects on their well-being and life experiences.

A short story. I was on the tube in central London at rush hour, making my way home one evening, and I decided to stand the whole way, which gave me the opportunity to observe other commuters as they traveled to their destinations. It was quite interesting what I observed of other passengers' behavior, and as it happens, it has helped me draw the conclusion discussed in this chapter. One gentleman sat not too far away from me and was staring down, so as not to make eye contact with fellow passengers seated opposite. As I continued to observe him from time to time, it was evident he had a lot on his mind, and the expressions on his face went from serious to smiling to worried and so on. He was clearly having a full-blown conversation in his mind and going from one state to another, affecting his moods. I am not a mind reader, but I could see he was rehearsing a previous experience for better or worse in his mind. At one point, he was moving his lips. Ignorant of anything about the Force in motion, he was giving focus and attention to his past event, and for sure, in the days, weeks, or months that followed, he would experience similar episodes in his reality once again.

Mental conversations are very powerful. As we process our thoughts and words in our minds, along with images, our conversations in our imagination begin to flow naturally.

Memories of a negative nature, which make us feel emotionally upset or annoyed, cause our thoughts to repeat as if on a loop, and we find ourselves talking in our minds with much intensity and clarity; it's as if we are playing out and experiencing the whole negative episode over and over again, using all the senses and our mind with great accuracy.

In the mind's eye, as we play the part of ourselves and the part of whoever was there at the time, we find ourselves changing the conversation so as to get our point across, to put the record straight, or to ensure we win the argument we feel we previously lost. We do this with the hope of setting the record straight and coming out the winner to satisfy the ego. When we realize it is just our imagination, we find that we aren't satisfied with that version of events, causing us to repeat the whole scene in our minds again and again on a loop, which can drive us a bit crazy, to say the least. Some of us get to a point where our conversations in the mind are spoken out loud, which makes us look a bit weird, especially if we are overheard by people nearby. You may have witnessed people in deep conversation with themselves. It looks peculiar, right? You've probably thought to yourself in an instant, "That person must be a head case." They speak as themselves out loud and answer in their minds as the other person in a full-blown conversation. We have all done it at some point when someone or something has really bothered us.

Speaking in one's mind can sometimes go on for long periods of time, and as we fixate on an issue that bothers us, we recycle it more and more.

The conversation can continue for hours, sometimes days, and as we continue to give such focus and attention to the issue, it can cause us a lot of stress and grief, which does not serve us well at all, as we are creating the very thing so it appears in our lives again and again. Depending on the emotional intensity of our imagination and mental speech, the whole episode will surely appear very quickly in our reality via the Force.

Remember, the Force is unbiased; it just reflects back in kind, as it always remains impartial but precise. It's a Force of infinite power, intelligence, and unprecedented organization beyond the mind's grasp.

If we want to ensure we avoid this kind of situation and we have full control of our mental speech in our imagination, we must practice observing our thoughts and conversations in our mind and be aware of what does and does not serve us. It does take time and a lot of practice, but eventually, you become aware, and by default, you will monitor your mental speech.

When we observe our mental conversations and thoughts in our imagination, keeping them positive, we are creating our very future via the Force. Just to remind ourselves, the Force is a power for good, but it can be a power for bad if not used correctly. It is one power. Use it for good and direct it to your desired goals. I have always believed we have the mental power to influence the flow of energy through controlled thinking and focused attention, and we can control the direction of the Force for anything we want in life. As already mentioned, we are all energy; everything in the universe is energy, and the thoughts we think are energy. We are not separate; we are all one, even though our senses deny this fact.

We know that when practicing the controlled imagination technique and the creative process with all the senses of reality including speech in the mind, we can effectively create up-and-coming attractions in our reality we wish to experience. Affirmations are also effective in creating too. The words we use are extremely powerful, and when used to affirm, statements of success, health, wealth, and happiness can produce great results, especially if repeated and we have total belief in what we are affirming. Thought and speech create emotions, which are feelings. Feelings are vibrations of energy, which emit a frequency via the Force. This frequency then creates and reflects back into our reality the very things we affirm and imagine in the days, weeks, or months to follow. How soon we experience them is down to the intensity of the emotions we experience while creating what we see, hear, and feel to be true in our imagination.

Our inner speech has a major influence on our attitude, and altering our inner conversations in our imagination will dramatically change our attitude, thus changing our experiences in our daily life. When we match our mental conversations with emotion to our goals and desires in life, we find that the creative Force delivers our desires and goals to us, fulfilled exactly how we envisaged them in our minds.

When we realize our dreams from this exercise, we feel the outcome was fate, luck, or meant to happen. We find it hard to comprehend at first that all things are generated from the energy of our imagination and conversations in the mind; but, once we believe it to be true and understand all things are energy, we can create the life we want and realize all things are possible. So if we don't like what's happening to us in life, we must change our mental conversations and remain focused on our renewed way of thought and speech. Always be aware of any negative circumstances that may lead you to stray and contaminate your thinking by returning you to a negative frame of mind, which, in turn, creates a life of negative experiences once more.

> All that we are is the result of what we have thought: it is
> founded on our thoughts and made up of our thoughts. If
> a man speaks or acts with an evil thought, suffering fol-
> lows him as the wheel follows the hoof of the beast that

draws the wagon...If a man speaks or acts with a good thought, happiness follows him like a shadow that never leaves him.

—Gautama Buddha

Man alone has the power to transform his thoughts into physical reality; man alone can dream and make his dreams come true.

—Napoleon Hill

The mind is like a magnifying glass; when focused, it will burn your desire into existence.

Readers notes

Chapter Sixteen

Famous People Who Have Used the Force

After establishing the correct way to perform the creative formula for achieving goals and desires, I realized that many famous people knew something about the creative process, and they created their life achievements through their imaginations and beliefs. Some knew what they were doing, but most did it by default.

Before I knew about the Force, I always wondered, with fascination, "Why them? Are they just lucky? Are they the chosen ones? Or is it their destiny?" With the knowledge I have now, I know that none of that was true. They were responsible for the lives they created for themselves. What they have or what they are in life is the effect, so they must be the cause, as we live in a cause-and-effect universe. The causation comes from the activity of our thoughts.

Elvis Presley, of whom I am a big fan, like many in this world, was a great example. It's been written, and you can hear him saying in some video clips, that all his dreams came true a hundred times over. His many great quotes refer to his dreams creating his life, not to mention his wealth, to take care of his mother. He had a very powerful imagination and also assumed the role, the image, and the mannerisms that he played out very clearly in his public appearances for all to see. He knew at a young age what he wanted and believed he was different and that something special would happen to him. He didn't know what at the time, but he knew something would happen for sure.

Alert Einstein also understood the imagination very well. He talked about imagination being more important than knowledge itself. He carried out several thought experiments with profound results.

The experiments of Dr. Masaru Emoto, a Japanese researcher, have been widely publicized on the Internet and in his books. He demonstrated in his experiments how our thoughts, feelings, and intentions alter the structure of water. When words of love, gratitude, and positive thoughts are directed toward a sample of water by way of focused meditation and attention, after freezing the water and observing it under a powerful microscope, we can see beautiful crystal formations. They are like snowflakes. Alternatively, if words of hate and negative thoughts are directed to a sample of water and it is frozen, we observe, using a high-powered microscope, that the water creates shapeless structures that don't have any crystal formations. It is in a state of disarray. So we know our thoughts are extremely powerful, and humans, being over 80 percent water, must choose our thoughts and words wisely for ourselves and for others, as we alter reality for better or for worse and that could be devastating to our health or to the health of another.

Other scientists carried out similar experiments on plants. These experiments were done at great distance apart; for example, the plants were in one country and the positive thoughts, words, and intentions from a team of people were sent out from another. The results were amazing. When viewed through a special camera, the leaves on the plants started to glow. It was as if the plants were in the same room where the experiments were performed; so it was established distance, space, time, and matter are no obstacle for thought energy, as we are all one and we are all connected in the universe.

Everything in the universe is energy. We are all one with life, and the person who can control his or her imagination can create anything he or she wants in life. Nothing is impossible.

Here are some great quotes on the power of thought:

"Ambition is a dream with a V8 engine."

—Elvis Presley

"From the time I was a kid, I always knew something was going to happen to me. Didn't know exactly what."

—Elvis Presley

"When I was a child, ladies and gentlemen, I was a dreamer. I read comic books, and I was the hero of the comic book. I saw movies, and I was the hero in the movie. So every dream I ever dreamed has come true a hundred times…"

—Elvis Presley

"The true sign of intelligence is not knowledge but imagination."

—Albert Einstein

"To raise new questions, new possibilities, to regard old problems from a new angle requires creative imagination and marks real advance in science."

—Albert Einstein

"Imagination is more important than knowledge. For knowledge is limited, whereas imagination embraces the entire world, stimulating progress, giving birth to evolution."

—Albert Einstein

In these quotes, we can see that Elvis created his life by default, because he used his wild imagination to create his future via the Force. Many accomplished singing artists to this day have been heard saying that when they were young, they used to parade in front of a mirror with a hairbrush in hand to simulate a microphone and imagine they were on stage performing in front of a live audience. Little did they know the power of the Force in bringing to life their very dream.

Albert Einstein fully understood the power of imagination and how thoughts create reality and shared his findings with the world.

Elvis and Albert Einstein shared common traits—gratitude and generosity. Elvis shared his wealth over and over with anyone he could in life. He gave away a great deal of money and material wealth to many, as he loved to see the expressions of delight on people's faces, and he changed the lives of many. You see, giving is an important habit to maintain in the creative process. Just as it is important to receive, it's equally important to give, to share, and to be of a generous nature. Failure to do so will not only prevent abundance appearing in your life, but what you already have will slowly be taken from you, so be aware you cannot utilize the creative process with the mind of a miser, as this mind-set carries with it a negative frequency. It's a common fact that tithing is a great way to start the process of giving in a more apt and consistent way, if one is not used to doing so.

Many people today are aware that thoughts create our reality and are using the process in their daily lives. The number is growing, thanks to the Internet and self-help pioneers in the world today and in the past.

A person is what he or she thinks about all day long.

—Ralph Waldo Emerson

Reality is merely an illusion, albeit a very persistent one.

—Albert Einstein

Readers notes

Chapter Seventeen

Warning

I feel it's my duty to advise you that the creative process should never be used to create negative situations or imagine harm for anyone or anything in life. Many people throughout history, whether by default or intentionally, have experienced bad karma from their actions and evil thoughts.

You see, when you have emotionalized thoughts playing out in your mind's eye in which harm is inflicted on another, you are setting yourself up for a negative backlash of unpleasant experiences. When anyone visualizes a negative outcome in life upon another, the negative intention returns to him or her in kind and usually when he or she least expects it with a lot of negative repercussions.

> If one imagines unlovely things for another, they are going
> to produce them—not in the other, but in themselves.

—Neville Goddard

The following is a true case study.

I had a person who worked for me in my business many years ago, and when we parted company, he set up his own business later in life, which I discovered was an unethical business. I advised him on countless occasions that what he was doing was not correct and would not serve him in the long run.

In short, he was receiving payments from clients and making false promises to provide a service to them with guarantees of success, knowing fully well it wasn't the case. Time went by, and eventually negative publicity came out about the nature of his business ethics and bad dealings.

I continued to warn him, as I felt he was misguided and blinded by the fact that what he thought he was doing was all aboveboard, because he was paying his taxes and creditors.

Well, not long after, and for obvious reasons I can't go into, the repercussions arrived and were immense. He suffered blow after blow and serious bad luck. What he took in one hand was taken from the other repeatedly.

Nature has a way of getting even, of balancing your books of life, should we say. It evens the situation out to correct itself. For every action, there is an equal and opposite reaction. You may have heard the saying based on Isaac Newton's third law of motion. For every cause, there is an effect.

A positive cause will create a positive effect, and a negative cause will create a negative effect.

You see, nature will not always take back the very thing you have taken from another by unethical means. You may be affected in many ways. For example, your health may suffer. You may lose something of great value or someone very dear to you, not necessarily through death but possibly through a breakup in a relationship with a partner or a close friend.

I believe from my own observation in life that the worse the negative intention or action committed, the worse the consequences you can expect to receive. It reminds me of a boomerang; it will spin back to the source every time. Some may think that there are people who get away with their negative actions or intentions. You may even have heard people say, "Crime pays." Well, it doesn't pay. No one gets away with any negative intention or action. The longer the boomerang is out there, spinning at a high velocity, the harder it will hit the person and knock him or her down in life with great force. However, some are ignorant of this fact and continue in life on the same destructive path, experiencing the wrath of their thoughts and actions over and over again. They just put it down to bad luck and move on with their lives if they can. For others, it's a wake-up call. They realize it's karma for their actions and do their best to make amends.

History has shown us over and over that powerful leaders who have abused their positions and violated the rights of others have always been met with defeat.

Never violate the rights of others for your own self-gain. Maintain integrity and mutual benefit to sustain good fortune, great health, and peace of mind, which is priceless.

So be warned. This creative process should only be used for the good of all and all that is good in life. If you feel you have been injured by someone in life, let it go and forgive that person. Never hijack anyone's karma. Leave him or her with it. Don't seek revenge or harbor malicious thoughts; it won't serve you well to do so. We live in a world of abundance, and you will be rewarded over and over for your good intentions and actions in life. (Refer to the chapter on "Forgiveness" for guidance.)

> How people treat you is their karma; how you react is yours.
>
> —Wayne Dyer

It is the combination of thought and love which forms the irresistible force of the law of attraction.

—Charles Hammel

You create your own universe as you go along.

—Winston Churchill

Readers notes

Chapter Eighteen

Challenge Your Reality

Some might ask, "How can I change my life when I get up every day and face the same story? The very story I feel stuck with? I feel trapped in a cycle of the same thing but a different day, and I don't have the extra money, wisdom, health, or courage to change anything."

I hear this story from my students time and time again. Well, as mentioned before, we are responsible for everything that has occurred in our lives thus far, and our lives are a reflection of who we really are. Change what you are, and things change; that's a fact. I have experienced it all my life. We do not have to be victims of circumstance. It's a choice, a mental choice we make, and we focus on it with all the senses of reality until it becomes an objective fact.

The experience of a negative mental pattern we hold in our imagination continues to expand. As long as we focus our imagination on it, it keeps us in a negative existence.

You see, when we keep observing our results in life and focus our attention and energy on them constantly, we create the same results— for example, the bad relationships, low bank account, boring job, poor health, and so on.

It's important not to take your unwanted current situation as fact. Remember your imagination has created your reality thus far. It is all different states of mind that we pass through on a daily basis, so ignore the facts.

If you are not satisfied with your life the way it is—for example, the job you are in; your relationship with your partner, friends, or family; your health condition; your financial situation; or whatever else for that matter—challenge your reality mentally. Refuse mentally to accept the situation as it is and live through it, but don't accept it. This may seem quite hard to do, especially when you are faced with the same state of affairs day in and day out; but, with practice, it becomes easier as you remain focused on the new desired status in your mind. You have to weather the storm, so to speak, until the effects of your previous thought patterns diminish and subside, and then you will begin to experience your new desires fulfilled from your creative sessions via the Force.

Start to use the creative process clearly laid out in this book and envisage in your mind's eye the situation you would ideally like to experience—the new job, partner, friends, health, financial situation, new business, or whatever you desire to have changed in your life. Don't settle for what you are now or what you have if you are not satisfied and fulfilled. Challenge your reality with your imagination and create your ideal life.

Always remember, everything in your world was first experienced in your mind, the gateway to infinite power, the Force. Every physical object around you was first an idea in the human imagination. Our thoughts are constantly changing our environment and experiences on a daily basis.

Change who you are for the better in your imagination, and you will experience a whole new world. I have seen it time and time again. It will feel like magic. I urge you to try it and see for yourself. You will be truly astonished. I have heard many a student say, "I can't believe it's that simple."

Our world is nothing but a virtual helmet operated by our human imagination.

Abundance is not something we acquire. It is something we tune into.

—Wayne Dyer

Readers notes

Chapter Nineteen

Summary and Recap of the Creative Process

I have outlined a few examples in this book of some desired goals fulfilled by me and my students. As a reminder, I covered how to get the perfect relationship, how to heal oneself, how to get that perfect job, how to obtain material wealth, and how to achieve many other things in life.

If it's a dream vacation you are wanting, I explain what you should do. Here is a perfect example. I got to talking with a neighbor of mine, and she brought up her desire to visit the Cayman Islands. Well, I told her that she should go, because it's a great place, and I shared with her all the great places I had visited, as I had spent a lot of time myself traveling and living in many parts of the world.

Anyway, the conversation went on, and she openly said, "I can't afford it. I just don't have the money right now."

I instantly replied, "Don't think of the money. Focus on being there and experiencing the whole trip as though you have already been there, and you shall be there. It will happen in the least expected way you could imagine."

At this point, as always, I was eager to share my knowledge with her. I always do to help people achieve their goals and desires in life. I told her

I had a great formula I used to achieve my desires in life, an
ears and very attentive while I explained to her what she sho

Let me run through what I shared with her for your benefit. If it's the
dream vacation or place you want to visit for a great break or maybe a
person dear to you whom you've not seen in a long while, this will truly be
of interest to you.

Right, as always, find the time to sit quietly in a chair or lie down at
night before you retire to sleep. As mentioned earlier, this is even better
because your mind is in a state of calm and awareness, which is perfect
for creating. It's that sleepy state of being before you drop off into a deep
sleep. So quiet your mind until you feel totally relaxed. Once you are feeling peaceful, begin to focus your mind's eye on the country or place you
wish to visit. See what you would see, for example, the surroundings,
the views from where you are standing, the people, nature, the buildings,
the vehicles, and all the details you can create. Hear the sounds, like
the different language spoken by the locals, the noise from the traffic,
and if you are by the sea, the surf, seagulls, and so on. Feel the warmth
of the sun and the breeze from the sea. Smell the salt in the air or the
scents of the local food from the restaurants nearby. Remember, you are
not an observer; you are you in this movie as you, seeing through your
own eyes, experiencing all this through your senses, as you would if it
were happening in real life. Reflect on your departure from where you
traveled, looking back at your trip coming over on the plane or ship. See
your home country in the distance, as far away from where you are now
in your mind's eye, and continue to create everything that would suggest
you are in the country or place you wish to be. As I said before, continue
to enjoy the feelings of these sessions day by day, until such time the
whole episode feels real and plays out before your very eyes. Always
challenge your reality; ignore your current state of affairs playing out on
your screen of life, and remain focused on your controlled daydream
with faith and belief that it's already happened and it's a done deal. As

for my neighbor, well, she was motivated to carry out the instructions, which she did over period of time, and she successfully won a holiday to Australia. She had already planned to go to Australia, and her trip was originally prebooked, so that freed up her savings from that holiday. She had the money available for her trip to the Cayman Islands. Well, she couldn't wait to tell me that she had booked a visit to the Cayman Islands. Her words were, "You won't believe it; it worked! I'm going to the Cayman Islands. It's all booked up."

I did say to her, "Wow! I knew it would work out for you." I told her at that point, "You not only went to the Cayman Islands, but you traveled business class." I said it deliberately in past tense, like it had already happened to assume the fulfilled desire.

The next time we met was after she got back from her trip, and she said to me, "I traveled business class!" It was unbelievable. Her friend's husband, who was a frequent flyer in business class, happened to be on the flight and decided, as a treat, to give up his business-class seat for her. She was overwhelmed by how the whole thing appeared and turned out for her. She even sent me a picture of herself sitting in business class on her flight before takeoff. She has since used the process for a trip to Disney World in Florida, and the results were just as phenomenal. She had acquired the money through a family inheritance, totally out of the blue. You see, the Force will bring it all together. Just know want you want, follow the process, believe, feel it's already happened, and then watch it show up.

Hearing the results of anyone who uses this practice always gives me goose bumps, a feeling of achievement, and yet again, confirmation that this philosophy and formula really does work, not only for me but for everyone. Remember this, controlled daydreaming is not wishful thinking. It is a creative process that is more intricate. It requires accurate thinking and attention to detail.

If it's a business you want to have, then carry out the same process, but of course change the movie—change the details and contents in your creative session. See yourself already in business, successful, and proud of your achievements. Give it all the senses of reality in your mind's eye during your creative session, as if it's already up and running and very successful; then continue until it becomes a fact in your reality. Remember, don't think and worry about how it's going to happen or the time frame in which it will appear. Everything has its own arrival date when it will appear in your life and different methods of achievement. Just know what you want and that your desire has already happened, and it will, if you carry out the creative process correctly.

Do you want that dream home you so wish to live in? If so, then visualize yourself in your mind's eye as already in that home, moving from room to room, with all the furnishings and decoration of your taste in such a home. Utilize the creative process as laid out in this book with all the sensations and feelings of living in your new home. Feel what it would feel like as you touch the furniture, door handles, drapes, and banisters of the stairways as you walk through your home. Picture your guests sitting in your living room, saying to you things like, "What a beautiful home you have!" and "How lucky you are to be living in such a house!" Give it all the details you would want to see in your dream home, and stay focused and committed to your controlled daydream until your desire presents itself to you in reality as we know it.

Never share your desires with anyone, as to do so will only dissipate your focus and invite comments and opinions that may plant the seed of doubt in your mind, disrupting the creative process via the Force to attaining your fulfilled desire.

Your mind is like a movie projector; if you don't like what's on your screen of life, then change the reels.

What things so ever ye desire, when ye pray, believe that ye receive them, and ye shall have them.

—Mark 11:24

Imagination is the beginning of creation. You imagine what you desire, you will what you imagine, and at last you create what you will.

—George Bernard Shaw

Readers notes

Chapter Twenty

Creating for Others

Imagination creates our reality, and knowing this, I often create the ideal desired outcome for those I know. If we can create using the Force for ourselves, we can most definitely use the formula to create for others, as everything is energy, and what is in your reality can be rehearsed and adjusted to create the desired outcome you wish to see for others in your world.

I've used it several times for family, friends, and anyone I felt could do with the help. A friend of mine had a house for sale, and he was in a bit of a dilemma, as he had committed to buying another home he wanted to move to but needed to sell his first. Many can relate to such a situation. It's very stressful, to say the least. Well, he rang me up, moaning about how many people had viewed his house with no sale and how his property had been on the market for a great length of time. He wondered what he was going to do, as he didn't want the seller of his next house to pull out of the deal. Anyway, when he finished speaking, I said in a positive manner, "Don't worry; it will all work out fine for you," and hung up the phone. Once off the phone, I carried out a creative session, rehearsing the whole phone call from start to finish in my imagination. I imagined him calling me up and sharing positive news about how he'd sold his house and couldn't wait to move to his new property. I added as much detail in the conversation as possible; for example, I wished him well and said things like, "I am pleased for you. Congratulations! I hope you like your new home." After this very brief session, I would do no more but believe. That was how the conversation really happened, totally ignoring the previous negative phone call. A couple of weeks later, I got a call from him, telling me he'd sold up and was preparing to move to his new home with joy and jubilation in his voice. I was very pleased for him and about the result I obtained from the session. It never ceases to amaze me how well it works.

You can change the story for anything you wish. It actually works better when you create for others, as there is no emotional block of self-doubt as there is when you do it for yourself. You believe it's already an objective fact; it's a done deal. You let it go, and the desire makes its appearance. You can tell the person what you did after the fact if you wish to—but not before, as it will affect the outcome. It always makes me feel great when I know someone's circumstances have turned out for the best. It's a feeling of goodwill.

Readers notes

A Final Thought

For great things to happen in life, you have to do great things. It may seem like a play on words, but that is how it is. As mentioned before, we live in a cause-and-effect universe, and every action has a reaction, so create the cause through thought and do the action in the physical world. It doesn't have to be something big; it can be a smile to a passerby or being courteous by opening the door for someone or giving up your seat on the bus for a mother or an elderly person. If you are in your car in traffic, let someone in the queue or give someone a free ride. You may compliment someone at work or show appreciation for what someone has done. There are many things in life we can say and do in a good way, and the great thing is, they are all positive actions that will not only make other people feel great but will make you feel even better. Only good experiences will be appear in your life via the Force.

I hope this book has a great effect on your life. You may find that you want to read this book over and over to grasp the concept of creating your life via the Force and to develop this skill to a fine art. I sincerely hope you have enjoyed reading this book as much as I have enjoyed writing it.

Live knowing, daydream often, be thankful, share the knowledge, and be happy!

About the Author

Nidal Saadeh is from the city of Bath, England. A college graduate in electrical engineering, he changed direction at a young age and spent many years traveling the globe, marketing resort properties, and later entered the financial industry. As a father first and foremost, as well as an entrepreneur, philanthropist, author, lecturer, and certified NLP (neurolinguistic programming) practitioner, he believes his calling is one of service to others. After many years of success in all areas of his life, he dedicates most of his time to helping others, his priority being his children and family. As an analytically minded person, he constantly studies books on mind power, self-help, new thought, metaphysics, and many other such fields, exploring why people, events, and circumstances appear in one's life. As a result of his findings and personal life-changing experiences, he decided to turn his hand to writing, to share his knowledge with the aim of reaching the masses and changing the lives of many. His fascination with how some people meet with adversity and struggle throughout their lives while others seem to have it all with little effort also intrigued him and convinced him to put pen to paper. Some of the many true life stories laid out in his book are a testament to his ongoing mentoring.

For more information visit www.createyourlifebyforce.com

Resources

Here are some authors that have influenced and inspired me in more ways than I could have imagined. You may wish to research and read further from these great authors and speakers in the personal-development industry. They have published many books, too many to list here.

Wallace D. Wattles.
Napoleon Hill.
Charles Francis Haanel.
Ernest Homes.
Prentice Mulford.
Joseph Murphy.
Catherine Ponder.
James Allen.
Neville Goddard.
Walter William Atkinson.

Suggested Reading and References

Wattles, Wallace *The Science of getting Rich*
Top of the Mountain Publishing, 1910

Hill, Napoleon (first edition 1937) *Think and Grow Rich*
Renaissance Books, 2001

Ponder, Catherine *Dynamic Law Prosperity*
DeVorss & Company, 1985

Murphy, Dr. Joseph (first edition 1963)
The Power of the Subconscious Mind
Martino Publishing, 2011

Atkinson, William Walter (first edition 1906)
Thought Vibration or The Law of Attraction in the Thought World
Kessinger Publishing Company, 1996

Goddard, Neville (first edition 1961)
The Law and the Promise
Martino Publishing, 2010

Made in the USA
Middletown, DE
15 June 2017